55 Asian Recipes for Home

By: Kelly Johnson

Table of Contents

Appetizers:

- Spring Rolls with Peanut Dipping Sauce
- Gyoza (Japanese Potstickers)
- Chicken Satay Skewers
- Vietnamese Fresh Spring Rolls with Shrimp
- Edamame with Sea Salt

Soups:

- Tom Yum Soup (Thai Hot and Sour Soup)
- Mis Soup with Tofu and Seaweed
- Hot and Sour Soup
- Wonton Soup
- Laksa (Spicy Malaysian Coconut Noodle Soup)

Salads:

- Thai Mango Salad with Peanut Dressing
- Japanese Seaweed Salad
- Chinese Chicken Salad
- Som Tum (Thai Green Papaya Salad)
- Kimchi Cucumber Salad

Main Dishes - Chicken:

- General Tso's Chicken
- Teriyaki Chicken
- Butter Chicken (Indian Murgh Makhani)
- Thai Basil Chicken (Pad Krapow Gai)
- Korean Fried Chicken

Main Dishes - Beef:

- Beef and Broccoli
- Bulgogi (Korean Grilled Beef)
- Massaman Curry with Beef

- Vietnamese Shaking Beef (Bo Luc Lac)
- Thai Drunken Noodles (Pad Kee Mao)

Main Dishes - Seafood:

- Shrimp Pad Thai
- Sweet and Sour Fish
- Szechuan Shrimp
- Malaysian Chili Crab
- Japanese Teriyaki Salmon

Main Dishes - Vegetarian:

- Tofu and Vegetable Stir-Fry
- Vegetable Biryani
- Eggplant with Garlic Sauce
- Japanese Okonomiyaki (Vegetable Pancake)

Rice and Noodle Dishes:

- Chicken Fried Rice
- PPad See Ew (Thai Stir-Fried Noodles)
- Pineapple Fried Rice
- Bibimbap (Korean Mixed Rice)
- Hainanese Chicken Rice

Curries:

- Thai Green Curry with Chicken
- Japanese Curry Rice
- Indian Vegetable Curry
- Panang Curry with Beef
- Malaysian Rendang Curry

Dim Sum:

- Har Gow (Shrimp Dumplings)
- Siu Mai (Pork and Shrimp Dumplings)
- Char Siu Bao (BBQ Pork Buns)
- Egg Custard Tarts
- Xiao Long Bao (Soup Dumplings)

Street Food:

- Pad Thai
- Banh Mi (Vietnamese Sandwich)
- Satay Noodles
- Japanese Takoyaki (Octopus Balls)
- Korean Street Toast

Appetizers:

Spring Rolls with Peanut Dipping Sauce

Ingredients:

For Spring Rolls:

- 8 to 10 rice paper wrappers
- 1 cup cooked and shredded chicken or tofu (for vegetarian option)
- 1 cup thinly sliced lettuce
- 1 cup thinly sliced cucumber
- 1 cup julienned carrots
- 1/2 cup fresh mint leaves
- 1/2 cup fresh cilantro leaves
- Rice vermicelli noodles, cooked according to package instructions

For Peanut Dipping Sauce:

- 1/2 cup peanut butter
- 3 tablespoons soy sauce
- 2 tablespoons rice vinegar
- 1 tablespoon sesame oil
- 1 tablespoon honey or maple syrup
- 1 clove garlic, minced
- 1 teaspoon grated ginger
- 2-3 tablespoons water (adjust for desired consistency)
- Crushed peanuts for garnish (optional)

Instructions:

For Spring Rolls:

Prepare all the filling ingredients and set them aside.
Fill a large shallow bowl with warm water. Dip one rice paper wrapper into the water for about 10 seconds until it becomes pliable.
Place the wet rice paper on a clean surface. Add a small portion of each filling ingredient, placing them in the center of the wrapper.

Fold the sides of the wrapper over the filling, then fold the bottom over the filling, and roll tightly to seal. Repeat the process for the remaining wrappers.
Arrange the spring rolls on a serving plate, seam side down.

For Peanut Dipping Sauce:

In a bowl, whisk together peanut butter, soy sauce, rice vinegar, sesame oil, honey or maple syrup, minced garlic, and grated ginger.
Add water gradually until you achieve the desired dipping sauce consistency.
Adjust the sweetness and saltiness according to your taste.
Pour the peanut dipping sauce into a serving bowl.

Assembly:

Serve the spring rolls on a platter with the peanut dipping sauce on the side.
Optionally, garnish the dipping sauce with crushed peanuts for added texture.
Enjoy your delicious spring rolls by dipping them into the flavorful peanut sauce!

These spring rolls are not only visually appealing but also a delightful combination of fresh vegetables, protein, and a tasty dipping sauce that will surely please your taste buds.

Gyoza (Japanese Potstickers)

Ingredients:

For the Gyoza Filling:

- 1 pound ground pork
- 1 cup napa cabbage, finely chopped
- 3 green onions, finely chopped
- 2 cloves garlic, minced
- 1 tablespoon ginger, grated
- 2 tablespoons soy sauce
- 1 tablespoon sesame oil
- 1 teaspoon sugar
- 1/2 teaspoon black pepper
- 1/4 cup water chestnuts, finely chopped (optional for added crunch)

For the Gyoza Wrapper:

- Gyoza or dumpling wrappers (round, thin)

For Dipping Sauce:

- 3 tablespoons soy sauce
- 1 tablespoon rice vinegar
- 1 teaspoon sesame oil
- 1 teaspoon sugar
- 1 green onion, finely chopped (optional for garnish)

For Cooking:

- 2 tablespoons vegetable oil
- 1/2 cup water

Instructions:

Preparing the Filling:

In a large bowl, combine ground pork, chopped napa cabbage, green onions, minced garlic, grated ginger, soy sauce, sesame oil, sugar, black pepper, and water chestnuts (if using).

Mix the ingredients thoroughly until well combined. Refrigerate the filling for about 30 minutes to let the flavors meld.

Assembling the Gyoza:

Place a small spoonful of the filling in the center of a gyoza wrapper.

Moisten the edge of the wrapper with water and fold it in half, creating a half-moon shape. Pinch the edges to seal.

Pleat the sealed edge, starting from one end and working your way to the other, creating a crescent shape. Press the edges together to ensure a tight seal.

Repeat the process until all the filling is used.

Cooking the Gyoza:

Heat vegetable oil in a large skillet over medium-high heat.

Arrange the gyoza in the skillet, flat side down, and cook until the bottoms become golden brown (about 2-3 minutes).

Carefully add water to the skillet, cover with a lid, and steam the gyoza for an additional 5-6 minutes, or until the filling is cooked through.

Remove the lid and let the gyoza cook uncovered until the water evaporates and the bottoms crisp up again.

Preparing the Dipping Sauce:

In a small bowl, mix soy sauce, rice vinegar, sesame oil, and sugar until well combined.

Garnish the dipping sauce with chopped green onions if desired.

Serving:

Serve the gyoza hot, with the dipping sauce on the side.

Enjoy the flavorful combination of the crispy bottom, tender filling, and the savory dipping sauce!

Gyoza makes for a delicious appetizer or a satisfying snack, and the process of making them can be a fun and interactive cooking activity.

Chicken Satay Skewers

Ingredients:

For the Marinade:

- 1.5 pounds boneless, skinless chicken thighs, cut into thin strips
- 1/4 cup soy sauce
- 2 tablespoons fish sauce
- 2 tablespoons honey
- 2 tablespoons vegetable oil
- 2 cloves garlic, minced
- 1 tablespoon ginger, grated
- 1 teaspoon ground coriander
- 1 teaspoon ground cumin
- 1/2 teaspoon turmeric

For Peanut Dipping Sauce:

- 1/2 cup creamy peanut butter
- 3 tablespoons soy sauce
- 2 tablespoons honey
- 1 tablespoon rice vinegar
- 1 teaspoon sesame oil
- 1 clove garlic, minced
- 1/2 teaspoon red pepper flakes (optional)
- Water to adjust consistency

For Skewers:

- Wooden skewers, soaked in water for at least 30 minutes

Instructions:

Marinating the Chicken:

In a bowl, combine soy sauce, fish sauce, honey, vegetable oil, minced garlic, grated ginger, ground coriander, ground cumin, and turmeric to create the marinade.

Add the chicken strips to the marinade, ensuring they are well coated. Marinate in the refrigerator for at least 1 hour or overnight for maximum flavor.

Making the Peanut Dipping Sauce:

In a separate bowl, whisk together peanut butter, soy sauce, honey, rice vinegar, sesame oil, minced garlic, and red pepper flakes if using.

Add water gradually until you achieve the desired dipping sauce consistency. Set aside.

Skewering and Grilling:

Preheat the grill or grill pan over medium-high heat.

Thread the marinated chicken strips onto the soaked wooden skewers.

Grill the chicken skewers for about 3-4 minutes per side, or until fully cooked and slightly charred.

Remove the skewers from the grill and let them rest for a few minutes.

Serving:

Arrange the chicken satay skewers on a serving platter.

Serve the peanut dipping sauce on the side.

Optionally, garnish with chopped fresh cilantro or chopped peanuts.

Enjoy these flavorful chicken satay skewers with the delicious peanut dipping sauce!

Chicken satay skewers are a crowd-pleaser and make for a fantastic appetizer or main course, especially when paired with the rich and savory peanut dipping sauce.

Vietnamese Fresh Spring Rolls with Shrimp

Ingredients:

For the Spring Rolls:

- 8 to 10 rice paper wrappers
- 16-20 medium-sized shrimp, cooked, peeled, and deveined
- 1 cup vermicelli rice noodles, cooked and cooled
- 1 cup bean sprouts
- 1 cucumber, julienned
- 1 carrot, julienned
- Fresh mint leaves
- Fresh cilantro leaves
- Lettuce leaves

For the Dipping Sauce:

- 1/4 cup hoisin sauce
- 2 tablespoons peanut butter
- 1 tablespoon soy sauce
- 1 tablespoon rice vinegar
- 1 teaspoon sriracha sauce (adjust to taste)
- 2 tablespoons water (adjust for desired consistency)

Instructions:

Preparing the Ingredients:

Cook the vermicelli rice noodles according to the package instructions. Drain and set aside to cool.
Cook the shrimp by boiling or sautéing until pink and opaque. Allow them to cool before using.
Julienne the cucumber and carrot into thin strips.

Assembling the Spring Rolls:

Fill a shallow dish with warm water. Dip one rice paper wrapper into the water for about 10 seconds or until it becomes pliable.

Place the wet rice paper on a clean surface. In the center of the wrapper, add a few shrimp, a handful of vermicelli noodles, bean sprouts, julienned cucumber, julienned carrot, mint leaves, cilantro leaves, and a lettuce leaf.

Fold the sides of the wrapper over the filling, then fold the bottom over the filling, and roll tightly to seal. Repeat the process for the remaining wrappers.

Arrange the fresh spring rolls on a serving plate, seam side down.

Making the Dipping Sauce:

In a bowl, whisk together hoisin sauce, peanut butter, soy sauce, rice vinegar, and sriracha sauce.

Add water gradually until you achieve the desired dipping sauce consistency.

Adjust the flavors to your liking.

Serving:

Serve the Vietnamese fresh spring rolls on a platter with the dipping sauce on the side.

Optionally, garnish the dipping sauce with chopped peanuts or a sprinkle of sesame seeds.

Enjoy these refreshing and flavorful spring rolls as a healthy appetizer or light meal!

These Vietnamese fresh spring rolls are not only delicious but also a vibrant and colorful addition to your table. The combination of fresh vegetables, shrimp, and the flavorful dipping sauce makes for a delightful and satisfying dish.

Edamame with Sea Salt

Ingredients:

- 2 cups fresh or frozen edamame in pods
- Sea salt, to taste

Instructions:

Boiling Edamame:

> Bring a pot of water to a boil. If using frozen edamame, follow the package instructions for boiling.
> Add the edamame pods to the boiling water.
> Boil fresh edamame for about 4-5 minutes or frozen edamame for 2-3 minutes, or until they are tender but still have a slight crunch.
> Drain the edamame in a colander and rinse them under cold water to stop the cooking process.

Seasoning with Sea Salt:

> Place the boiled edamame in a serving bowl.
> Sprinkle sea salt over the edamame, starting with a pinch and adjusting according to your taste preferences.
> Toss the edamame gently to ensure that the sea salt is evenly distributed.
> Serve the edamame with an extra sprinkle of sea salt on top or provide additional salt on the side for individual preference.

Serving:

> Serve the edamame as a snack, appetizer, or side dish.
> Optionally, garnish with a wedge of lime for added citrus flavor.
> Enjoy the edamame by popping the beans out of the pods with your fingers or teeth.

Note: You can also serve edamame with flavored sea salt or additional seasonings like garlic powder, chili flakes, or sesame seeds for extra flavor.

This simple edamame with sea salt recipe is a quick and healthy snack that is not only delicious but also packed with protein and nutrients. It's a great option for parties, gatherings, or as a light and nutritious appetizer.

Soups:

Tom Yum Soup (Thai Hot and Sour Soup)

Ingredients:

For the Broth:

- 4 cups chicken or vegetable broth
- 2 lemongrass stalks, bruised and cut into 2-inch pieces
- 3 kaffir lime leaves
- 3-4 slices galangal or ginger
- 3 Thai bird's eye chilies, smashed (adjust to taste)
- 2 cloves garlic, minced
- 1 medium-sized onion, thinly sliced
- 1 medium-sized tomato, cut into wedges
- 200g (7 oz) shrimp, peeled and deveined
- 200g (7 oz) mushrooms, sliced
- 1 cup cherry tomatoes
- 1 tablespoon fish sauce
- 1 tablespoon soy sauce (optional, for vegetarian version)
- 1 tablespoon lime juice
- 1 teaspoon sugar

Optional Ingredients:

- 200g (7 oz) chicken, thinly sliced (if not making a vegetarian version)
- 100g (3.5 oz) tofu, cubed (for vegetarian version)

Garnish:

- Fresh cilantro leaves
- Thai bird's eye chilies, sliced
- Lime wedges

Instructions:

In a large pot, bring the chicken or vegetable broth to a simmer.

Add lemongrass, kaffir lime leaves, galangal or ginger, Thai bird's eye chilies, minced garlic, sliced onion, and tomato wedges to the pot. Allow it to simmer for 10-15 minutes to infuse the flavors.

If not making a vegetarian version, add thinly sliced chicken to the pot and cook until it's no longer pink.

Add shrimp to the pot and cook until they turn pink and opaque.

Stir in sliced mushrooms, cherry tomatoes, fish sauce, soy sauce (if using), lime juice, and sugar. Allow the soup to simmer for an additional 5-7 minutes until the vegetables are tender.

Taste the soup and adjust the seasoning according to your preference by adding more fish sauce, lime juice, or sugar if needed.

Remove lemongrass stalks, kaffir lime leaves, and galangal or ginger slices from the soup before serving.

Ladle the Tom Yum soup into bowls and garnish with fresh cilantro leaves, sliced Thai bird's eye chilies, and lime wedges.

Serve the Tom Yum soup hot and enjoy the spicy, tangy, and aromatic flavors!

This Tom Yum soup recipe is a classic Thai dish that's both comforting and invigorating. Adjust the level of spiciness and sourness according to your taste preferences. It's a delightful soup that works well as a starter or a light meal on its own.

Mis Soup with Tofu and Seaweed

Ingredients:

- 4 cups dashi (Japanese fish or vegetable stock)
- 3 tablespoons miso paste (white or red, according to preference)
- 200g (7 oz) firm tofu, cubed
- 2 tablespoons dried wakame seaweed, rehydrated
- 2 green onions, thinly sliced
- 1 tablespoon soy sauce (optional, adjust to taste)
- 1 teaspoon mirin (optional, for a touch of sweetness)
- 1 teaspoon sesame oil (optional)
- 1 sheet nori (seaweed), cut into thin strips (for garnish)

Instructions:

In a saucepan, bring the dashi to a gentle simmer. If you don't have dashi, you can use vegetable stock as a substitute.

In a small bowl, dilute the miso paste with a few tablespoons of the hot dashi until it forms a smooth paste.

Add the diluted miso paste back into the saucepan with the simmering dashi. Stir well to combine.

Add tofu cubes to the soup and let it simmer for about 2-3 minutes until the tofu is heated through.

Rehydrate the dried wakame seaweed in warm water according to package instructions. Once rehydrated, add the wakame to the soup.

If desired, add soy sauce and mirin to the soup for additional flavor. Adjust the seasoning according to your taste.

Optional: Drizzle sesame oil into the soup for an extra layer of flavor.

Just before serving, add thinly sliced green onions to the soup.

Ladle the miso soup into bowls and garnish with thin strips of nori seaweed. Serve hot and enjoy the comforting and savory Miso Soup with Tofu and Seaweed!

Note: Be cautious with the amount of soy sauce as miso paste itself is salty. Adjust the quantity based on your taste preferences.

This Miso Soup with Tofu and Seaweed is not only delicious but also a nourishing and comforting dish. It's a classic Japanese soup that makes for a perfect appetizer or a light meal on its own.

Hot and Sour Soup

Ingredients:

- 8 cups chicken or vegetable broth
- 200g (7 oz) firm tofu, julienned
- 1/2 cup bamboo shoots, thinly sliced
- 1/2 cup shiitake mushrooms, thinly sliced
- 1/2 cup wood ear mushrooms, rehydrated and thinly sliced
- 1/4 cup rice vinegar
- 3 tablespoons soy sauce
- 1 tablespoon sesame oil
- 1 teaspoon sugar
- 1 teaspoon white pepper (adjust to taste)
- 1/2 teaspoon chili oil or Sriracha sauce (adjust to taste)
- 2 eggs, beaten
- 2 tablespoons cornstarch, dissolved in 3 tablespoons water
- 1/4 cup green onions, thinly sliced
- 1/4 cup cilantro, chopped (for garnish)

Instructions:

In a large pot, bring the chicken or vegetable broth to a simmer over medium heat.
Add tofu, bamboo shoots, shiitake mushrooms, and wood ear mushrooms to the simmering broth. Cook for about 5-7 minutes until the mushrooms are tender.
In a small bowl, mix together rice vinegar, soy sauce, sesame oil, sugar, white pepper, and chili oil or Sriracha.
Pour the seasoning mixture into the pot and stir well. Adjust the seasoning to taste.
Slowly pour the beaten eggs into the soup while stirring gently to create ribbons of cooked egg.
In a separate bowl, dissolve cornstarch in water to create a slurry. Gradually add the slurry to the soup while stirring continuously to thicken the soup.
Once the soup has thickened, reduce the heat to low and let it simmer for an additional 2-3 minutes.
Add sliced green onions to the soup, reserving some for garnish.
Ladle the hot and sour soup into bowls, garnish with chopped cilantro and the remaining green onions.

Serve immediately and enjoy the comforting and flavorful Hot and Sour Soup!

Adjust the level of spiciness and sourness according to your taste preferences. This classic Chinese soup is a delicious and warming option, perfect for a light meal or as an appetizer.

Wonton Soup

Ingredients:

For the Wontons:

- 1/2 pound ground pork
- 1/4 pound peeled and deveined shrimp, finely chopped
- 2 tablespoons soy sauce
- 1 tablespoon sesame oil
- 2 teaspoons fresh ginger, grated
- 2 green onions, finely chopped
- 1 egg
- Wonton wrappers (square or round)

For the Soup:

- 8 cups chicken or vegetable broth
- 2 teaspoons soy sauce
- 1 tablespoon sesame oil
- 2 teaspoons fresh ginger, grated
- 2 garlic cloves, minced
- 2 cups baby bok choy, chopped
- 1 cup shiitake mushrooms, sliced
- 1 carrot, julienned
- 1 tablespoon rice vinegar (optional)
- Salt and white pepper to taste

For Garnish:

- Green onions, thinly sliced
- Cilantro leaves, chopped

Instructions:

Making the Wonton Filling:

In a bowl, combine ground pork, chopped shrimp, soy sauce, sesame oil, grated ginger, chopped green onions, and egg.

Mix the ingredients until well combined.

Place a small amount of the wonton filling in the center of each wonton wrapper.

Moisten the edges of the wrapper with water and fold it over the filling, creating a triangle or any desired shape. Press the edges to seal.

Making the Soup:

In a large pot, bring the chicken or vegetable broth to a simmer over medium heat.

Add soy sauce, sesame oil, grated ginger, and minced garlic to the simmering broth. Allow it to simmer for about 5 minutes to infuse the flavors.

Add baby bok choy, shiitake mushrooms, and julienned carrot to the broth. Cook for an additional 3-5 minutes until the vegetables are tender.

Optionally, add rice vinegar for a touch of acidity. Adjust salt and white pepper to taste.

Cooking the Wontons:

Bring a separate pot of water to a boil.

Drop the wontons into the boiling water and cook for 4-5 minutes or until they float to the surface and are cooked through.

Using a slotted spoon, transfer the cooked wontons to the prepared soup.

Serving:

Ladle the Wonton Soup into bowls, ensuring each bowl has a mix of broth, vegetables, and wontons.

Garnish with sliced green onions and chopped cilantro.

Serve hot and enjoy this comforting and flavorful Wonton Soup!

This homemade Wonton Soup is a delightful combination of savory broth, tender vegetables, and delicious wontons. It's a perfect dish for warming up on a chilly day or as a comforting appetizer.

Laksa (Spicy Malaysian Coconut Noodle Soup)

Ingredients:

For the Laksa Paste:

- 3 stalks lemongrass, white part only, thinly sliced
- 4 shallots, peeled and roughly chopped
- 4 cloves garlic, peeled
- 1 thumb-sized piece of ginger, peeled and sliced
- 3 red chilies, deseeded and chopped
- 1 tablespoon coriander seeds
- 1 teaspoon turmeric powder
- 1 tablespoon chili paste or sambal oelek
- 2 tablespoons vegetable oil

For the Laksa Soup:

- 2 tablespoons vegetable oil
- 200g (7 oz) chicken, thinly sliced (or tofu for a vegetarian version)
- 200g (7 oz) shrimp, peeled and deveined
- 4 cups chicken or vegetable broth
- 1 can (14 oz) coconut milk
- 2 tablespoons fish sauce (or soy sauce for a vegetarian version)
- 1 tablespoon brown sugar
- Salt to taste
- 200g (7 oz) rice vermicelli noodles, cooked according to package instructions
- Bean sprouts, lime wedges, cilantro, and sliced red chilies for garnish

Instructions:

Preparing the Laksa Paste:

In a food processor, combine lemongrass, shallots, garlic, ginger, red chilies, coriander seeds, turmeric powder, and chili paste or sambal oelek.
Pulse the ingredients until a smooth paste forms.

Heat vegetable oil in a pan, add the laksa paste, and sauté over medium heat for 5-7 minutes until fragrant. Set aside.

Making the Laksa Soup:

In a large pot, heat vegetable oil over medium heat. Add the laksa paste and cook for 2-3 minutes.
Add chicken (or tofu) and shrimp to the pot, and cook until the chicken is no longer pink and the shrimp turn pink and opaque.
Pour in chicken or vegetable broth, coconut milk, fish sauce (or soy sauce), and brown sugar. Stir well and let it simmer for 10-15 minutes.
Adjust the seasoning with salt according to taste.

Assembling the Laksa:

Place a portion of cooked rice vermicelli noodles in serving bowls.
Ladle the hot laksa soup over the noodles.
Garnish with bean sprouts, lime wedges, cilantro, and sliced red chilies.
Serve immediately and enjoy the bold and spicy flavors of Malaysian Laksa!

This Laksa recipe offers a rich and aromatic coconut broth with a perfect balance of spice. It's a comforting and satisfying soup that brings the vibrant flavors of Malaysia to your table.

Salads:

Thai Mango Salad with Peanut Dressing

Ingredients:

For the Salad:

- 2 ripe mangoes, peeled, pitted, and julienned
- 1 red bell pepper, thinly sliced
- 1 cucumber, julienned
- 1 carrot, julienned
- 1/2 red onion, thinly sliced
- 1/4 cup fresh cilantro leaves, chopped
- 1/4 cup fresh mint leaves, chopped
- 1/4 cup roasted peanuts, chopped

For the Peanut Dressing:

- 3 tablespoons peanut butter
- 2 tablespoons soy sauce
- 2 tablespoons rice vinegar
- 1 tablespoon sesame oil
- 1 tablespoon honey or maple syrup
- 1 teaspoon grated ginger
- 1 clove garlic, minced
- 1 tablespoon water (optional, to adjust consistency)

Instructions:

Preparing the Salad:

In a large bowl, combine julienned mangoes, red bell pepper, cucumber, carrot, red onion, cilantro, and mint.
Toss the ingredients gently to combine and evenly distribute the colors.
Sprinkle chopped roasted peanuts over the salad for added crunch.

Making the Peanut Dressing:

In a small bowl, whisk together peanut butter, soy sauce, rice vinegar, sesame oil, honey or maple syrup, grated ginger, and minced garlic.

If the dressing is too thick, add water gradually until you achieve the desired consistency. Whisk well to combine.

Taste the dressing and adjust the sweetness or saltiness according to your preference.

Assembling the Salad:

Drizzle the peanut dressing over the prepared salad.
Toss the salad gently to coat the ingredients with the peanut dressing.
Optional: Garnish with additional chopped peanuts, cilantro, and mint.
Serve the Thai Mango Salad immediately, or refrigerate until ready to serve.

Note: You can also add grilled chicken, shrimp, or tofu to make it a complete meal.

This Thai Mango Salad with Peanut Dressing is a refreshing and vibrant dish that showcases the perfect balance of sweet, savory, and tangy flavors. It's a delightful salad that can be enjoyed on its own or as a side to complement your favorite Thai-inspired meals.

Japanese Seaweed Salad

Ingredients:

- 1/2 cup dried wakame seaweed
- 1 tablespoon soy sauce
- 1 tablespoon rice vinegar
- 1 tablespoon sesame oil
- 1 teaspoon sugar
- 1 teaspoon grated ginger
- 1 teaspoon sesame seeds
- 1/2 cucumber, thinly sliced
- 1/4 cup thinly sliced red radishes
- 1/4 cup julienned carrots
- 2 tablespoons chopped green onions (scallions)
- 1 teaspoon mirin (optional)
- 1 teaspoon sake (optional)

Instructions:

Rehydrating the Wakame:
- Place the dried wakame seaweed in a bowl and cover it with cold water.
- Allow the seaweed to rehydrate for about 10-15 minutes or until it becomes tender.
- Drain and squeeze out any excess water.

Preparing the Dressing:
- In a small bowl, whisk together soy sauce, rice vinegar, sesame oil, sugar, grated ginger, sesame seeds, mirin (if using), and sake (if using).

Assembling the Salad:
- In a large bowl, combine the rehydrated wakame seaweed, thinly sliced cucumber, sliced radishes, julienned carrots, and chopped green onions.

Adding the Dressing:
- Pour the dressing over the salad ingredients.

Tossing the Salad:
- Gently toss the salad until the ingredients are well coated with the dressing.

Chilling the Salad:

- Place the seaweed salad in the refrigerator and let it chill for at least 30 minutes before serving.

Serving:
- Serve the Japanese Seaweed Salad chilled.

Optional Garnish:
- Garnish with additional sesame seeds or chopped green onions before serving.

This Japanese Seaweed Salad is not only refreshing but also packed with umami flavors. It makes a great side dish for sushi or any Japanese-inspired meal. The combination of wakame seaweed, crisp vegetables, and the savory-sweet dressing creates a delicious and healthy salad.

Chinese Chicken Salad

Ingredients:

For the Salad:

- 2 cups shredded cooked chicken breast
- 4 cups shredded Napa cabbage
- 1 cup shredded red cabbage
- 1 cup shredded carrots
- 1 red bell pepper, thinly sliced
- 1 cup mandarin orange segments, drained
- 1/2 cup sliced almonds, toasted
- 1/4 cup chopped cilantro
- 1/4 cup chopped green onions (scallions)

For the Dressing:

- 3 tablespoons soy sauce
- 2 tablespoons rice vinegar
- 1 tablespoon sesame oil
- 1 tablespoon honey
- 1 teaspoon grated ginger
- 1 clove garlic, minced
- 1 teaspoon sesame seeds (optional)

Instructions:

Preparing the Salad:

In a large bowl, combine shredded cooked chicken, Napa cabbage, red cabbage, shredded carrots, sliced red bell pepper, mandarin orange segments, toasted sliced almonds, chopped cilantro, and chopped green onions.
Toss the ingredients gently until well combined.

Making the Dressing:

In a small bowl, whisk together soy sauce, rice vinegar, sesame oil, honey, grated ginger, and minced garlic.
Optional: Add sesame seeds to the dressing for an extra layer of flavor.
Taste the dressing and adjust the sweetness or saltiness according to your preference.

Assembling the Salad:

Drizzle the dressing over the salad.
Toss the salad until the ingredients are evenly coated with the dressing.
Optional: Garnish with additional cilantro, green onions, or toasted sliced almonds.
Serve the Chinese Chicken Salad immediately, or refrigerate until ready to serve.

Note: You can also add crispy wonton strips for added crunch.

This Chinese Chicken Salad is a delightful combination of crisp vegetables, tender chicken, and a flavorful dressing. It's a refreshing and satisfying salad that can be enjoyed as a light meal on its own or as a side dish to complement your favorite Chinese dishes.

Som Tum (Thai Green Papaya Salad)

Ingredients:

For the Salad:

- 2 cups shredded green papaya
- 1 cup cherry tomatoes, halved
- 1/2 cup long beans or green beans, cut into 2-inch pieces
- 2-3 Thai bird's eye chilies, minced (adjust to taste)
- 2 cloves garlic, minced
- 1/4 cup roasted peanuts, coarsely chopped
- 2 tablespoons dried shrimp, optional (soaked and drained, omit for vegetarian version)
- 1-2 tablespoons fish sauce (or soy sauce for vegetarian version)
- 1 tablespoon palm sugar or brown sugar
- 1 lime, juiced

For Garnish:

- Fresh cilantro leaves
- Additional roasted peanuts

Instructions:

Prepping the Ingredients:
- Peel and shred the green papaya using a julienne peeler or a box grater.
- If using long beans, cut them into 2-inch pieces.
- Halve the cherry tomatoes.

Making the Salad:
- In a large mortar and pestle, pound minced garlic and Thai bird's eye chilies together to release their flavors.
- Add the shredded green papaya, cherry tomatoes, and long beans to the mortar. Use a spoon to toss the ingredients while pounding gently.
- Add dried shrimp (if using), fish sauce, palm sugar, and lime juice. Continue pounding and tossing until well combined.

- Taste the salad and adjust the flavors by adding more fish sauce, sugar, or lime juice according to your preference.

Finishing Touches:
- Add coarsely chopped roasted peanuts and toss them into the salad.

Serving:
- Transfer the Som Tum to a serving plate or bowl.
- Garnish with fresh cilantro leaves and additional roasted peanuts.
- Serve immediately as a refreshing side dish or with sticky rice.

Note: Som Tum can be served as is or with grilled chicken or shrimp for a more substantial meal.

This Thai Green Papaya Salad (Som Tum) offers a burst of flavors – the crunch of papaya, the heat of chilies, the sweetness of palm sugar, and the savory notes from fish sauce. It's a classic Thai dish that makes a perfect side or a light and vibrant meal.

Kimchi Cucumber Salad

Ingredients:

- 2 English cucumbers, thinly sliced
- 1 cup Napa cabbage kimchi, chopped
- 2 green onions, thinly sliced
- 1 tablespoon sesame seeds, toasted (optional, for garnish)

For the Dressing:

- 2 tablespoons soy sauce
- 1 tablespoon rice vinegar
- 1 tablespoon sesame oil
- 1 tablespoon honey or maple syrup
- 1 teaspoon grated ginger
- 1 clove garlic, minced
- 1 teaspoon gochugaru (Korean red pepper flakes, optional, for extra heat)

Instructions:

Preparing the Cucumbers:
- Wash the English cucumbers and thinly slice them. You can use a mandoline for even slices.

Chopping the Kimchi:
- Chop the Napa cabbage kimchi into smaller pieces. If the kimchi is too large, it may be beneficial to cut it into bite-sized portions.

Making the Dressing:
- In a small bowl, whisk together soy sauce, rice vinegar, sesame oil, honey or maple syrup, grated ginger, minced garlic, and gochugaru (if using).

Assembling the Salad:
- In a large bowl, combine the sliced cucumbers, chopped kimchi, and thinly sliced green onions.
- Pour the dressing over the cucumber and kimchi mixture.
- Toss the salad gently to ensure that the cucumbers and kimchi are evenly coated with the dressing.

Chilling the Salad:

- Refrigerate the Kimchi Cucumber Salad for at least 15-20 minutes before serving. This allows the flavors to meld and intensify.

Serving:
- Before serving, sprinkle toasted sesame seeds over the salad for a nutty flavor and extra texture.
- Serve the Kimchi Cucumber Salad as a refreshing side dish or as a complement to Korean meals.

Note: Adjust the level of spiciness by varying the amount of gochugaru, and customize the sweetness according to your taste preferences.

This Kimchi Cucumber Salad offers a delightful combination of crunchy cucumbers, tangy kimchi, and a savory-sweet dressing. It's a quick and easy side dish that brings the bold flavors of Korean cuisine to your table.

Main Dishes - Chicken:

General Tso's Chicken

Ingredients:

For the Chicken:

- 1.5 lbs boneless, skinless chicken thighs or breasts, cut into bite-sized pieces
- 1 cup cornstarch
- 2 eggs, beaten
- Vegetable oil for frying

For the Sauce:

- 1/4 cup soy sauce
- 2 tablespoons rice vinegar
- 2 tablespoons hoisin sauce
- 2 tablespoons sugar
- 1 tablespoon cornstarch
- 1/2 cup chicken broth

For Stir-Fry:

- 2 tablespoons vegetable oil
- 3 cloves garlic, minced
- 1 tablespoon ginger, grated
- 1/2 teaspoon red pepper flakes (adjust to taste)
- 3 green onions, chopped
- Sesame seeds for garnish (optional)

Instructions:

Coating and Frying the Chicken:

In a bowl, coat the chicken pieces with cornstarch until evenly covered.

Dip each cornstarch-coated chicken piece into the beaten eggs, ensuring it's well coated.

In a large pan or wok, heat vegetable oil over medium-high heat for frying.

Fry the chicken pieces in batches until golden brown and crispy. Remove and place them on a paper towel-lined plate to drain excess oil.

Making the Sauce:

In a small bowl, whisk together soy sauce, rice vinegar, hoisin sauce, sugar, cornstarch, and chicken broth.

Stir-Frying:

In a clean pan or wok, heat 2 tablespoons of vegetable oil over medium heat.

Add minced garlic, grated ginger, and red pepper flakes. Stir-fry for about 30 seconds until fragrant.

Pour the prepared sauce into the pan and bring it to a simmer.

Once the sauce thickens slightly, add the fried chicken pieces to the pan. Toss until the chicken is well-coated with the sauce.

Add chopped green onions and toss again to combine.

Garnish with sesame seeds if desired.

Serving:

Serve General Tso's Chicken over steamed rice or noodles.

Optionally, garnish with additional chopped green onions and sesame seeds.

Enjoy this flavorful and slightly spicy Chinese-American classic!

Note: Adjust the level of spiciness by adding more or fewer red pepper flakes. You can also customize the sweetness by adjusting the amount of sugar in the sauce.

Teriyaki Chicken

Ingredients:

For the Teriyaki Sauce:

- 1/2 cup soy sauce
- 1/4 cup mirin
- 2 tablespoons sake or dry white wine
- 2 tablespoons brown sugar
- 1 teaspoon grated ginger
- 2 cloves garlic, minced
- 1 tablespoon cornstarch (optional, for thickening)

For the Chicken:

- 1.5 lbs boneless, skinless chicken thighs or breasts, cut into bite-sized pieces
- Salt and pepper to taste
- 2 tablespoons vegetable oil
- Sesame seeds and chopped green onions for garnish (optional)

Instructions:

Making the Teriyaki Sauce:

In a small saucepan, combine soy sauce, mirin, sake or white wine, brown sugar, grated ginger, and minced garlic.
Bring the mixture to a simmer over medium heat. Let it simmer for about 5 minutes, allowing the flavors to meld.
If you prefer a thicker sauce, mix cornstarch with a tablespoon of water to create a slurry. Add the slurry to the sauce and stir until it thickens. Remove from heat.

Cooking the Chicken:

Season the chicken pieces with salt and pepper.
In a large skillet or wok, heat vegetable oil over medium-high heat.
Add the seasoned chicken pieces to the hot skillet. Cook until browned on all sides and cooked through.
Once the chicken is cooked, pour the teriyaki sauce over the chicken in the skillet. Toss the chicken in the sauce until well-coated and heated through.

Serving:

    Serve Teriyaki Chicken over steamed rice or noodles.
    Garnish with sesame seeds and chopped green onions if desired.
    Enjoy this delicious homemade Teriyaki Chicken!

Note: You can add stir-fried vegetables such as broccoli, bell peppers, or carrots for a complete meal. Adjust the sweetness or saltiness of the teriyaki sauce according to your taste preferences.

Butter Chicken (Indian Murgh Makhani)

Ingredients:

For the Marinade:

- 1.5 lbs (700g) boneless, skinless chicken thighs or breasts, cut into bite-sized pieces
- 1 cup plain yogurt
- 1 tablespoon ginger paste
- 1 tablespoon garlic paste
- 1 teaspoon turmeric powder
- 1 teaspoon chili powder
- 1 teaspoon garam masala
- 1 teaspoon ground coriander
- 1 teaspoon cumin
- Salt to taste

For the Sauce:

- 2 tablespoons ghee or unsalted butter
- 1 large onion, finely chopped
- 2 tablespoons tomato paste
- 1 can (14 oz) crushed tomatoes
- 1 teaspoon ginger paste
- 1 teaspoon garlic paste
- 1 teaspoon garam masala
- 1 teaspoon ground coriander
- 1 teaspoon cumin
- 1/2 teaspoon turmeric powder
- 1/2 teaspoon chili powder (adjust to taste)
- 1 cup heavy cream
- Salt and sugar to taste

For Finishing:

- 2 tablespoons ghee or unsalted butter

- 1 teaspoon dried fenugreek leaves (kasuri methi)
- Fresh cilantro leaves, chopped (for garnish)
- Cooked basmati rice or naan (for serving)

Instructions:

Marinating the Chicken:

In a bowl, combine yogurt, ginger paste, garlic paste, turmeric powder, chili powder, garam masala, ground coriander, cumin, and salt.
Add the chicken pieces to the marinade, ensuring they are well-coated. Cover and refrigerate for at least 2 hours, preferably overnight.

Cooking the Chicken:

Preheat the oven to 400°F (200°C).
Thread the marinated chicken pieces onto skewers and place them on a baking tray. Bake for about 15-20 minutes or until the chicken is cooked through.
Alternatively, you can grill the chicken or cook it on a stovetop grill pan.

Making the Sauce:

In a large pan, heat ghee or butter over medium heat. Add chopped onions and sauté until golden brown.
Add ginger paste and garlic paste. Sauté for a minute until the raw smell disappears.
Stir in garam masala, ground coriander, cumin, turmeric powder, and chili powder. Cook for 1-2 minutes.
Add tomato paste and crushed tomatoes. Cook the mixture for about 10 minutes, stirring occasionally.
Pour in heavy cream and cook for an additional 5-7 minutes until the sauce thickens.
Season the sauce with salt and sugar according to your taste.

Finishing the Dish:

Add the baked or grilled chicken pieces to the sauce. Simmer for an additional 10-15 minutes, allowing the flavors to meld.

In a separate small pan, melt ghee or butter. Add dried fenugreek leaves (kasuri methi) and toast them for a minute.

Pour the fenugreek-infused ghee over the Butter Chicken and stir gently.

Garnish with chopped cilantro leaves.

Serve the Butter Chicken over basmati rice or with naan.

Enjoy this rich and flavorful Indian Butter Chicken with its creamy tomato-based sauce and aromatic spices!

Thai Basil Chicken (Pad Krapow Gai)

Ingredients:

- 1 lb (450g) ground chicken or thinly sliced chicken breast
- 2 tablespoons vegetable oil
- 4 cloves garlic, minced
- 3-4 Thai bird's eye chilies, minced (adjust to taste)
- 1 cup fresh Thai basil leaves
- 1 tablespoon fish sauce
- 1 tablespoon oyster sauce
- 1 tablespoon soy sauce
- 1 teaspoon sugar
- 1/4 cup chicken broth or water
- Fried egg (optional, for serving)
- Cooked jasmine rice (for serving)

Instructions:

Preparing Ingredients:
- If using ground chicken, ensure it is properly thawed if frozen. If using chicken breast, thinly slice it into bite-sized pieces.
- Mince garlic and Thai bird's eye chilies.
- Pick fresh Thai basil leaves.

Making the Sauce:
- In a small bowl, mix together fish sauce, oyster sauce, soy sauce, and sugar. Set aside.

Stir-Frying:
- Heat vegetable oil in a wok or large skillet over medium-high heat.
- Add minced garlic and Thai bird's eye chilies. Stir-fry for about 30 seconds until fragrant.
- Add ground chicken or sliced chicken breast to the wok. Break apart the ground chicken or cook the chicken slices until browned and cooked through.

Adding Sauce and Thai Basil:
- Pour the prepared sauce over the cooked chicken. Stir well to coat the chicken in the sauce.
- Add chicken broth or water to the wok. Continue stirring and simmering for an additional 2-3 minutes.

- Add fresh Thai basil leaves to the wok. Toss until the basil wilts and is evenly distributed.

Serving:
- Serve Pad Krapow Gai over jasmine rice.
- Optionally, top with a fried egg for an extra layer of flavor.
- Enjoy this quick and flavorful Thai Basil Chicken!

Note: Adjust the level of spiciness by adding more or fewer Thai bird's eye chilies. You can also use holy basil if Thai basil is not available for a more authentic flavor.

Korean Fried Chicken

Ingredients:

For the Chicken:

- 2 lbs (about 1 kg) chicken wings or drumettes
- Salt and pepper to taste
- 1 cup buttermilk
- 1 cup all-purpose flour
- Vegetable oil for frying

For the Sauce:

- 1/4 cup gochujang (Korean red pepper paste)
- 3 tablespoons soy sauce
- 2 tablespoons honey
- 2 tablespoons rice vinegar
- 2 teaspoons sesame oil
- 4 cloves garlic, minced
- 1 teaspoon grated ginger
- Sesame seeds and chopped green onions for garnish

Instructions:

Preparing the Chicken:

> Season the chicken wings or drumettes with salt and pepper.
> Place the seasoned chicken in a bowl and pour buttermilk over it. Ensure the chicken is well-coated. Let it marinate for at least 30 minutes, or refrigerate it for a few hours for better flavor absorption.
> Remove the chicken from the buttermilk and let the excess liquid drip off.
> In a separate bowl, dredge the chicken in all-purpose flour, ensuring each piece is evenly coated.

Frying the Chicken:

Heat vegetable oil in a deep fryer or a large, deep skillet to 350°F (175°C).
Fry the chicken in batches for about 10-12 minutes or until golden brown and crispy. Ensure the chicken is cooked through.
Remove the fried chicken and place it on a paper towel-lined plate to drain excess oil.

Making the Sauce:

In a saucepan, combine gochujang, soy sauce, honey, rice vinegar, sesame oil, minced garlic, and grated ginger.
Heat the sauce over medium heat, stirring until it thickens slightly and the ingredients are well combined.

Coating the Chicken:

Toss the fried chicken in the prepared sauce until each piece is evenly coated.
Garnish with sesame seeds and chopped green onions.
Serve the Korean Fried Chicken hot and enjoy!

Note: Adjust the level of spiciness by varying the amount of gochujang according to your preference. You can also serve the chicken with pickled radishes or coleslaw on the side for a refreshing contrast.

Main Dishes - Beef:

Beef and Broccoli

Ingredients:

For the Beef Marinade:

- 1 lb (about 450g) flank steak, thinly sliced against the grain
- 3 tablespoons soy sauce
- 1 tablespoon oyster sauce
- 1 tablespoon rice wine or dry sherry
- 1 tablespoon cornstarch
- 1 teaspoon sesame oil
- 1 teaspoon sugar
- 1/2 teaspoon black pepper

For the Stir-Fry:

- 2 tablespoons vegetable oil
- 3 cloves garlic, minced
- 1 teaspoon ginger, grated
- 4 cups broccoli florets
- 1/2 cup beef broth
- 3 tablespoons soy sauce
- 1 tablespoon oyster sauce
- 1 tablespoon hoisin sauce
- 1 tablespoon cornstarch mixed with 2 tablespoons water (for thickening)
- Cooked white rice for serving

Instructions:

Marinating the Beef:

In a bowl, combine sliced flank steak with soy sauce, oyster sauce, rice wine, cornstarch, sesame oil, sugar, and black pepper. Mix well, ensuring the beef is coated evenly. Let it marinate for at least 20-30 minutes.

Stir-Frying:

Heat 1 tablespoon of vegetable oil in a wok or large skillet over high heat.
Add the marinated beef to the hot wok, spreading it out to ensure even cooking.
Stir-fry for 1-2 minutes or until the beef is browned and cooked through. Remove the beef from the wok and set it aside.
In the same wok, add another tablespoon of vegetable oil.
Add minced garlic and grated ginger to the wok. Stir-fry for about 30 seconds until fragrant.
Add broccoli florets to the wok and stir-fry for 2-3 minutes until they are crisp-tender.
Pour beef broth into the wok and cover with a lid. Allow the broccoli to steam for an additional 2-3 minutes until fully cooked.
Return the cooked beef to the wok with the broccoli.

Making the Sauce:

In a small bowl, mix soy sauce, oyster sauce, hoisin sauce, and the cornstarch-water mixture.
Pour the sauce over the beef and broccoli in the wok.
Stir everything together until the sauce thickens and coats the beef and broccoli evenly.

Serving:

Serve Beef and Broccoli over cooked white rice.
Enjoy this classic and flavorful Chinese-American dish!

Note: Feel free to customize the vegetables or adjust the sauce according to your taste preferences. You can add a sprinkle of sesame seeds or sliced green onions as a garnish for extra flavor.

Bulgogi (Korean Grilled Beef)

Ingredients:

For the Marinade:

- 1.5 lbs (about 700g) thinly sliced beef (ribeye or sirloin)
- 1/2 cup soy sauce
- 1/4 cup pear juice or pureed pear
- 3 tablespoons brown sugar
- 2 tablespoons mirin (rice wine)
- 1 tablespoon sesame oil
- 4 cloves garlic, minced
- 1 tablespoon grated ginger
- 1 tablespoon sesame seeds
- 2 green onions, finely chopped
- Black pepper to taste

For Grilling:

- Vegetable oil for greasing the grill or pan
- Sliced green onions and toasted sesame seeds for garnish

Optional Toppings:

- Sliced green onions
- Sesame seeds
- Kimchi
- Lettuce leaves for wrapping

Instructions:

Preparing the Marinade:

In a bowl, combine soy sauce, pear juice or pureed pear, brown sugar, mirin, sesame oil, minced garlic, grated ginger, sesame seeds, chopped green onions, and black pepper.

Whisk the marinade until the sugar is fully dissolved.
Add the thinly sliced beef to the marinade, ensuring each piece is well-coated.
Cover the bowl and marinate in the refrigerator for at least 30 minutes, preferably 2-4 hours, or overnight for maximum flavor.

Grilling the Bulgogi:

Preheat a grill or grill pan over medium-high heat.
Lightly grease the grill or pan with vegetable oil to prevent sticking.
Grill the marinated beef slices for 2-3 minutes on each side or until they are cooked through and have a nice caramelized exterior.
Optionally, you can cook the beef in a skillet or wok on the stovetop if a grill is not available.

Serving:

Garnish the Bulgogi with sliced green onions and toasted sesame seeds.
Serve it over steamed rice, with lettuce leaves for wrapping, or alongside your favorite Korean side dishes.
Optional: Top with additional sliced green onions, sesame seeds, and serve with kimchi.
Enjoy the delicious and savory Korean Bulgogi!

Note: Bulgogi is often served with a side of rice, but you can also enjoy it in lettuce wraps or as part of a bibimbap bowl. Feel free to customize the toppings and accompaniments according to your preferences.

Massaman Curry with Beef

Ingredients:

For the Massaman Curry Paste:

- 4 dried red chilies, soaked in warm water
- 1 small onion, chopped
- 4 cloves garlic
- 1 thumb-sized piece of galangal or ginger, chopped
- 1 lemongrass stalk, sliced
- 1 teaspoon ground coriander
- 1 teaspoon ground cumin
- 1/2 teaspoon ground cinnamon
- 1/2 teaspoon ground cloves
- 1/2 teaspoon ground cardamom
- 1/2 teaspoon ground nutmeg
- 1/4 teaspoon black pepper
- 1 tablespoon shrimp paste (optional, omit for a vegetarian version)

For the Massaman Curry:

- 1.5 lbs (about 700g) beef stew meat, cut into bite-sized cubes
- 2 cans (28 oz) coconut milk
- 2-3 tablespoons massaman curry paste (adjust to taste)
- 2 tablespoons vegetable oil
- 2 tablespoons tamarind paste
- 2 tablespoons palm sugar or brown sugar
- 3-4 potatoes, peeled and cut into chunks
- 1 onion, sliced
- 1/2 cup roasted peanuts
- Fish sauce or soy sauce to taste
- Fresh cilantro leaves for garnish
- Cooked jasmine rice for serving

Instructions:

Preparing the Massaman Curry Paste:

In a blender or food processor, combine soaked dried red chilies, chopped onion, garlic, galangal or ginger, lemongrass, ground coriander, ground cumin, ground cinnamon, ground cloves, ground cardamom, ground nutmeg, black pepper, and shrimp paste (if using).

Blend until a smooth paste is formed. Add a little water if needed to facilitate blending.

Making the Massaman Curry:

Heat vegetable oil in a large pot over medium heat.
Add 2-3 tablespoons of the prepared massaman curry paste to the pot. Stir and cook for a couple of minutes until fragrant.
Add the beef cubes to the pot and brown them on all sides.
Pour in the coconut milk and bring the mixture to a simmer.
Add tamarind paste, palm sugar or brown sugar, sliced onions, and potato chunks to the pot. Stir well.
Cover the pot and let it simmer on low heat for about 1.5 to 2 hours or until the beef is tender.
Add roasted peanuts to the curry and season with fish sauce or soy sauce to taste.
Simmer for an additional 10-15 minutes until the flavors meld.

Serving:

Serve Massaman Curry over cooked jasmine rice.
Garnish with fresh cilantro leaves.
Enjoy the rich and flavorful Massaman Curry with Beef!

Note: You can customize the level of spiciness by adjusting the amount of curry paste.

Additionally, you can add other vegetables like carrots or bell peppers to the curry if desired.

Vietnamese Shaking Beef (Bo Luc Lac)

Ingredients:

For the Marinade:

- 1.5 lbs (about 700g) beef sirloin or tenderloin, cut into bite-sized cubes
- 3 cloves garlic, minced
- 1 tablespoon oyster sauce
- 1 tablespoon soy sauce
- 1 tablespoon fish sauce
- 1 tablespoon sugar
- 1 teaspoon black pepper

For the Stir-Fry:

- 2 tablespoons vegetable oil
- 1 red onion, cut into wedges
- 1-2 red or green bell peppers, sliced
- Cherry tomatoes, halved
- 2 tablespoons unsalted butter

For the Dipping Sauce:

- Lime wedges
- Salt and pepper

For Serving:

- Sliced cucumbers and tomatoes
- Cooked jasmine rice

Instructions:

Marinating the Beef:

In a bowl, combine the beef cubes with minced garlic, oyster sauce, soy sauce, fish sauce, sugar, and black pepper. Mix well and let it marinate for at least 30 minutes.

Stir-Frying:

Heat vegetable oil in a wok or large skillet over high heat.
Add the marinated beef cubes to the hot wok. Spread them out to ensure even cooking.
Let the beef sear without stirring for about 1-2 minutes until it develops a crust.
Stir and continue cooking until the beef is browned and cooked to your desired doneness. Remove the beef from the wok and set it aside.
In the same wok, add the unsalted butter. Stir in the red onion wedges and sliced bell peppers. Cook for about 2-3 minutes until they are slightly softened but still crisp.
Add the cooked beef back to the wok and toss everything together until well combined.

Preparing the Dipping Sauce:

Squeeze lime wedges into a small bowl.
Season the lime juice with salt and pepper. Mix well to create a simple dipping sauce.

Serving:

Serve Vietnamese Shaking Beef over cooked jasmine rice.
Arrange sliced cucumbers and tomatoes on the side.
Drizzle the beef with the dipping sauce or serve the sauce on the side.
Enjoy this flavorful and vibrant Vietnamese dish!

Note: Bo Luc Lac is often served on a sizzling platter for an added presentation.

Customize the vegetables and adjust the seasoning according to your taste preferences.

Thai Drunken Noodles (Pad Kee Mao)

Ingredients:

For the Noodles:

- 8 oz (about 225g) wide rice noodles
- 2 tablespoons vegetable oil
- 3 cloves garlic, minced
- 2 Thai bird's eye chilies, minced (adjust to taste)
- 1/2 lb (about 225g) chicken, beef, or shrimp, sliced
- 1 bell pepper, sliced
- 1 cup Thai basil leaves

For the Sauce:

- 3 tablespoons soy sauce
- 1 tablespoon oyster sauce
- 1 tablespoon fish sauce
- 1 tablespoon dark soy sauce
- 1 tablespoon sugar
- 1 teaspoon rice vinegar

For Garnish:

- Sliced red chili (optional)
- Lime wedges

Instructions:

Preparing the Noodles:

Cook the wide rice noodles according to the package instructions. Drain and set aside.

Making the Sauce:

In a bowl, mix together soy sauce, oyster sauce, fish sauce, dark soy sauce, sugar, and rice vinegar. Set aside.

Stir-Frying:

- Heat vegetable oil in a wok or large skillet over medium-high heat.
- Add minced garlic and minced Thai bird's eye chilies. Stir-fry for about 30 seconds until fragrant.
- Add sliced chicken, beef, or shrimp to the wok. Cook until the protein is fully cooked and slightly browned.
- Push the cooked meat to the side of the wok. Add a bit more oil if needed.
- Crack the egg into the wok and scramble it until it's almost fully cooked.
- Add sliced bell peppers to the wok and stir everything together.
- Add the cooked rice noodles to the wok.
- Pour the prepared sauce over the noodles. Toss everything together until the noodles are well-coated and heated through.
- Add Thai basil leaves to the wok and toss until they wilt.

Serving:

- Serve Thai Drunken Noodles hot.
- Garnish with sliced red chili if desired.
- Serve with lime wedges on the side for squeezing over the noodles.
- Enjoy the delicious and spicy flavors of Pad Kee Mao!

Note: Adjust the level of spiciness by varying the amount of Thai bird's eye chilies. You can also customize the protein and vegetables according to your preferences.

Main Dishes - Seafood:

Shrimp Pad Thai

Ingredients:

For the Pad Thai Sauce:

- 3 tablespoons tamarind paste
- 2 tablespoons fish sauce
- 1 tablespoon soy sauce
- 1 tablespoon oyster sauce
- 1 tablespoon brown sugar
- 1 teaspoon chili sauce (adjust to taste)

For the Pad Thai:

- 8 oz (about 225g) rice stick noodles
- 2 tablespoons vegetable oil
- 1/2 lb (about 225g) shrimp, peeled and deveined
- 2 cloves garlic, minced
- 2 eggs, lightly beaten
- 1 cup bean sprouts
- 2 green onions, sliced
- 1/4 cup crushed peanuts
- Lime wedges for serving
- Fresh cilantro for garnish

Instructions:

Preparing the Sauce:

In a small bowl, whisk together tamarind paste, fish sauce, soy sauce, oyster sauce, brown sugar, and chili sauce. Set aside.

Cooking the Rice Noodles:

Cook the rice stick noodles according to the package instructions. Drain and set aside.

Stir-Frying:

Heat vegetable oil in a wok or large skillet over medium-high heat.
Add minced garlic and stir-fry for about 30 seconds until fragrant.
Add shrimp to the wok and cook until they turn pink and opaque.
Push the shrimp to one side of the wok and pour the beaten eggs into the other side. Scramble the eggs until they are almost fully cooked.
Add the cooked rice noodles to the wok.
Pour the prepared Pad Thai sauce over the noodles and toss everything together.
Add bean sprouts and sliced green onions to the wok. Toss until the ingredients are well combined.
Stir in crushed peanuts.

Serving:

Serve Shrimp Pad Thai hot.
Garnish with lime wedges and fresh cilantro.
Enjoy this classic Thai dish with the perfect balance of sweet, sour, and savory flavors!

Note: Customize the level of spiciness by adjusting the amount of chili sauce. You can also add extra lime wedges and more crushed peanuts for added freshness and crunch.

Sweet and Sour Fish

Ingredients:

For the Sweet and Sour Sauce:

- 1/4 cup ketchup
- 3 tablespoons rice vinegar
- 2 tablespoons soy sauce
- 2 tablespoons brown sugar
- 1 tablespoon honey
- 1 tablespoon cornstarch (mixed with 2 tablespoons water)
- 1/2 cup pineapple juice (from canned pineapple)

For the Fish:

- 1 lb (about 450g) white fish fillets (tilapia, cod, or snapper), cut into bite-sized pieces
- Salt and pepper to taste
- 1/2 cup all-purpose flour
- Vegetable oil for frying

For Stir-Frying:

- 1 tablespoon vegetable oil
- 1 bell pepper, sliced
- 1 onion, sliced
- 1 cup pineapple chunks (fresh or canned)
- 1 carrot, thinly sliced
- 2 cloves garlic, minced
- 1 teaspoon ginger, grated

For Garnish:

- Sliced green onions
- Sesame seeds (optional)

Instructions:

Making the Sweet and Sour Sauce:

In a bowl, combine ketchup, rice vinegar, soy sauce, brown sugar, honey, and pineapple juice.
Mix well until the sugar is fully dissolved.
In a small saucepan, heat the sauce over medium heat. Once it starts to simmer, add the cornstarch-water mixture and stir until the sauce thickens. Remove from heat and set aside.

Preparing the Fish:

Season the fish fillets with salt and pepper.
Dredge the fish in all-purpose flour, shaking off any excess.
Heat vegetable oil in a deep fryer or a large skillet over medium-high heat.
Fry the fish pieces until they are golden brown and cooked through. Remove and place them on a paper towel-lined plate to drain excess oil.

Stir-Frying:

In a wok or large skillet, heat 1 tablespoon of vegetable oil over medium heat.
Add minced garlic and grated ginger. Stir-fry for about 30 seconds until fragrant.
Add sliced bell pepper, onion, carrot, and pineapple chunks to the wok. Stir-fry for 2-3 minutes until the vegetables are slightly tender.
Pour the prepared sweet and sour sauce over the vegetables. Stir to combine.
Add the fried fish pieces to the wok. Gently toss until the fish is coated with the sweet and sour sauce.

Serving:

Serve Sweet and Sour Fish over steamed rice.
Garnish with sliced green onions and sesame seeds if desired.
Enjoy this flavorful and vibrant sweet and sour dish!

Note: Adjust the sweetness or tanginess of the sauce according to your taste preferences. You can also add more vegetables such as snow peas or broccoli for added texture and color.

Szechuan Shrimp

Ingredients:

For the Marinade:

- 1 lb (about 450g) large shrimp, peeled and deveined
- 1 tablespoon soy sauce
- 1 tablespoon Shaoxing wine or dry sherry
- 1 teaspoon cornstarch

For the Sauce:

- 3 tablespoons soy sauce
- 2 tablespoons black vinegar
- 1 tablespoon hoisin sauce
- 1 tablespoon oyster sauce
- 1 tablespoon sugar

For Stir-Frying:

- 2 tablespoons vegetable oil
- 3 cloves garlic, minced
- 1 tablespoon ginger, grated
- 2 teaspoons Szechuan peppercorns, crushed
- 1 teaspoon red pepper flakes (adjust to taste)
- 1 bell pepper, sliced
- 1/2 cup unsalted roasted peanuts
- Sliced green onions for garnish

Instructions:

Marinating the Shrimp:

In a bowl, combine shrimp with soy sauce, Shaoxing wine or dry sherry, and cornstarch. Mix well and let it marinate for at least 15-20 minutes.

Making the Sauce:

In a small bowl, whisk together soy sauce, black vinegar, hoisin sauce, oyster sauce, and sugar. Set aside.

Stir-Frying:

Heat vegetable oil in a wok or large skillet over medium-high heat.
Add minced garlic and grated ginger to the wok. Stir-fry for about 30 seconds until fragrant.
Add crushed Szechuan peppercorns and red pepper flakes to the wok. Stir-fry for an additional 30 seconds.
Add sliced bell pepper to the wok and stir-fry for 2-3 minutes until slightly tender.
Push the vegetables to the side of the wok. Add the marinated shrimp and cook until they turn pink and opaque.
Pour the prepared sauce over the shrimp and vegetables. Toss everything together until the shrimp is well-coated.
Add unsalted roasted peanuts to the wok and stir to combine.

Serving:

Serve Szechuan Shrimp hot.
Garnish with sliced green onions.
Enjoy this spicy and flavorful Szechuan dish over steamed rice!

Note: Adjust the level of spiciness by varying the amount of red pepper flakes and Szechuan peppercorns according to your preference. You can also add more vegetables such as broccoli or snap peas for added color and texture.

Malaysian Chili Crab

Ingredients:

For the Crab:

- 2 large mud crabs, cleaned and cut into pieces
- 2 tablespoons vegetable oil
- 1 onion, finely chopped
- 4 cloves garlic, minced
- 1 thumb-sized ginger, grated
- 2 tablespoons chili paste (sambal oelek)
- 1 cup tomato puree
- 1 cup chicken or seafood broth
- 2 tablespoons soy sauce
- 1 tablespoon oyster sauce
- 1 tablespoon sugar
- Salt and pepper to taste

For Garnish:

- Fresh cilantro leaves
- Sliced green onions

For Serving:

- Steamed rice or crusty bread

Instructions:

Preparing the Crab:

Clean the mud crabs, removing the top shell and cutting them into pieces.

Making the Chili Crab:

Heat vegetable oil in a large wok or skillet over medium heat.

Add chopped onions, minced garlic, and grated ginger. Sauté until fragrant.

Stir in chili paste (sambal oelek) and cook for another minute.

Add the crab pieces to the wok, stirring to coat them in the aromatic mixture.

Pour in tomato puree, chicken or seafood broth, soy sauce, oyster sauce, sugar, salt, and pepper. Mix well.

Bring the mixture to a simmer and cover the wok. Let it cook for about 15-20 minutes or until the crab is fully cooked and the sauce has thickened.

Adjust the seasoning with additional salt, sugar, or soy sauce according to your taste.

Serving:

Transfer the Malaysian Chili Crab to a serving dish.

Garnish with fresh cilantro leaves and sliced green onions.

Serve the chili crab hot over steamed rice or with crusty bread to soak up the delicious sauce.

Enjoy this flavorful and spicy Malaysian dish!

Note: It's advisable to use a crab cracker and pick to enjoy the crab meat fully. Adjust the level of spiciness by adding more or less chili paste based on your preference.

Japanese Teriyaki Salmon

Ingredients:

For the Teriyaki Sauce:

- 1/4 cup soy sauce
- 2 tablespoons mirin
- 2 tablespoons sake or dry white wine
- 2 tablespoons brown sugar
- 1 teaspoon grated ginger
- 1 teaspoon grated garlic

For the Salmon:

- 4 salmon fillets (about 6 oz each)
- Salt and black pepper to taste
- 1 tablespoon vegetable oil
- Sesame seeds and sliced green onions for garnish

Instructions:

Making the Teriyaki Sauce:

In a small saucepan, combine soy sauce, mirin, sake or white wine, brown sugar, grated ginger, and grated garlic.
Heat the mixture over medium heat, stirring constantly until the sugar dissolves and the sauce thickens slightly. Remove from heat and set aside.

Preparing the Salmon:

Season the salmon fillets with salt and black pepper.
In a skillet or non-stick pan, heat vegetable oil over medium-high heat.
Place the salmon fillets in the pan, skin side down. Sear for 2-3 minutes until the skin is crispy.
Flip the salmon fillets and cook for an additional 2-3 minutes on the other side until they are golden brown.

Teriyaki Glazing:

Pour the prepared teriyaki sauce over the salmon fillets.
Allow the sauce to simmer and coat the salmon for an additional 2-3 minutes until the salmon is cooked through and glazed with the sauce.

Serving:

Transfer the Teriyaki Salmon to serving plates.
Garnish with sesame seeds and sliced green onions.
Serve the salmon over steamed rice or with your favorite vegetables.
Enjoy this delicious and savory Japanese Teriyaki Salmon!

Note: You can also broil or bake the salmon in the oven and then brush it with the teriyaki sauce for the last few minutes of cooking for a slightly different preparation. Adjust the sweetness or saltiness of the teriyaki sauce according to your taste preference.

Main Dishes - Vegetarian:

Tofu and Vegetable Stir-Fry

Ingredients:

For the Stir-Fry Sauce:

- 3 tablespoons soy sauce
- 2 tablespoons hoisin sauce
- 1 tablespoon rice vinegar
- 1 tablespoon sesame oil
- 1 tablespoon cornstarch (mixed with 2 tablespoons water)
- 1 tablespoon brown sugar
- 1 teaspoon grated ginger
- 2 cloves garlic, minced

For the Stir-Fry:

- 14 oz (about 400g) extra-firm tofu, pressed and cut into cubes
- 2 tablespoons vegetable oil
- 1 broccoli crown, cut into florets
- 1 bell pepper, sliced
- 1 carrot, julienned
- 1 zucchini, sliced
- 1 cup snap peas, trimmed
- 1 cup mushrooms, sliced
- 1 cup baby corn, halved
- Cooked rice or noodles for serving

Instructions:

Making the Stir-Fry Sauce:

> In a bowl, whisk together soy sauce, hoisin sauce, rice vinegar, sesame oil, cornstarch-water mixture, brown sugar, grated ginger, and minced garlic. Set aside.

Preparing the Tofu:

Press the tofu to remove excess water by placing it between paper towels and using a heavy object on top. Cut the tofu into cubes.
Heat 1 tablespoon of vegetable oil in a large wok or skillet over medium-high heat.
Add the tofu cubes and stir-fry until they are golden brown on all sides. Remove from the wok and set aside.

Stir-Frying the Vegetables:

In the same wok, add another tablespoon of vegetable oil.
Add broccoli florets, sliced bell pepper, julienned carrot, sliced zucchini, snap peas, mushrooms, and baby corn. Stir-fry for 3-5 minutes until the vegetables are crisp-tender.

Combining Tofu and Vegetables:

Add the cooked tofu back to the wok with the stir-fried vegetables.
Pour the prepared stir-fry sauce over the tofu and vegetables. Toss everything together until well-coated and heated through.

Serving:

Serve the Tofu and Vegetable Stir-Fry over cooked rice or noodles.
Garnish with sesame seeds or chopped green onions if desired.
Enjoy this healthy and flavorful tofu and vegetable dish!

Note: Feel free to customize the vegetables based on your preferences or what's in season. Adjust the sauce ingredients to achieve the desired balance of flavors.

Vegetable Biryani

Ingredients:

For the Stir-Fry Sauce:

- 3 tablespoons soy sauce
- 2 tablespoons hoisin sauce
- 1 tablespoon rice vinegar
- 1 tablespoon sesame oil
- 1 tablespoon cornstarch (mixed with 2 tablespoons water)
- 1 tablespoon brown sugar
- 1 teaspoon grated ginger
- 2 cloves garlic, minced

For the Stir-Fry:

- 14 oz (about 400g) extra-firm tofu, pressed and cut into cubes
- 2 tablespoons vegetable oil
- 1 broccoli crown, cut into florets
- 1 bell pepper, sliced
- 1 carrot, julienned
- 1 zucchini, sliced
- 1 cup snap peas, trimmed
- 1 cup mushrooms, sliced
- 1 cup baby corn, halved
- Cooked rice or noodles for serving

Instructions:

Making the Stir-Fry Sauce:

> In a bowl, whisk together soy sauce, hoisin sauce, rice vinegar, sesame oil, cornstarch-water mixture, brown sugar, grated ginger, and minced garlic. Set aside.

Preparing the Tofu:

> Press the tofu to remove excess water by placing it between paper towels and using a heavy object on top. Cut the tofu into cubes.

Heat 1 tablespoon of vegetable oil in a large wok or skillet over medium-high heat.

Add the tofu cubes and stir-fry until they are golden brown on all sides. Remove from the wok and set aside.

Stir-Frying the Vegetables:

In the same wok, add another tablespoon of vegetable oil.

Add broccoli florets, sliced bell pepper, julienned carrot, sliced zucchini, snap peas, mushrooms, and baby corn. Stir-fry for 3-5 minutes until the vegetables are crisp-tender.

Combining Tofu and Vegetables:

Add the cooked tofu back to the wok with the stir-fried vegetables.

Pour the prepared stir-fry sauce over the tofu and vegetables. Toss everything together until well-coated and heated through.

Serving:

Serve the Tofu and Vegetable Stir-Fry over cooked rice or noodles.

Garnish with sesame seeds or chopped green onions if desired.

Enjoy this healthy and flavorful tofu and vegetable dish!

Note: Feel free to customize the vegetables based on your preferences or what's in season. Adjust the sauce ingredients to achieve the desired balance of flavors.

Eggplant with Garlic Sauce

Ingredients:

For the Sauce:

- 3 tablespoons soy sauce
- 2 tablespoons rice vinegar
- 1 tablespoon hoisin sauce
- 1 tablespoon sugar
- 1 teaspoon cornstarch (mixed with 2 teaspoons water)
- 1 teaspoon sesame oil

For the Stir-Fry:

- 2 medium-sized eggplants, cut into bite-sized pieces
- Salt for sprinkling
- 3 tablespoons vegetable oil
- 4 cloves garlic, minced
- 1 tablespoon ginger, grated
- 2 green onions, sliced
- 1 tablespoon chili garlic sauce (adjust to taste)
- Sesame seeds and sliced green onions for garnish

Instructions:

Preparing the Eggplant:

Place the eggplant pieces in a colander and sprinkle with salt. Toss to coat and let them sit for about 15-20 minutes. This helps remove excess moisture and bitterness from the eggplant.
Rinse the salted eggplant pieces and pat them dry with a paper towel.

Making the Sauce:

In a bowl, whisk together soy sauce, rice vinegar, hoisin sauce, sugar, cornstarch-water mixture, and sesame oil. Set aside.

Stir-Frying:

Heat vegetable oil in a large wok or skillet over medium-high heat.
Add minced garlic and grated ginger to the wok. Stir-fry for about 30 seconds until fragrant.
Add the eggplant pieces to the wok and stir-fry for 5-7 minutes until they are golden brown and tender.
Push the eggplant to one side of the wok. Add sliced green onions and chili garlic sauce to the other side. Stir-fry for an additional 1-2 minutes.

Combining Eggplant with Sauce:

Pour the prepared sauce over the eggplant and green onions in the wok.
Toss everything together until the eggplant is well-coated with the garlic sauce.

Serving:

Serve Eggplant with Garlic Sauce hot.
Garnish with sesame seeds and additional sliced green onions.
Enjoy this flavorful and savory eggplant dish over steamed rice!

Note: Adjust the spiciness of the dish by varying the amount of chili garlic sauce. You can also add other vegetables like bell peppers or snow peas for additional flavor and texture.

Japanese Okonomiyaki (Vegetable Pancake)

Ingredients:

For the Batter:

- 2 cups all-purpose flour
- 1 1/2 cups dashi (Japanese soup stock)
- 2 eggs
- 1/2 head cabbage, thinly shredded
- 2 green onions, finely chopped
- 1/2 cup tenkasu (tempura scraps) or tempura flakes
- 1/2 cup cooked and chopped squid or shrimp (optional)
- Salt and pepper to taste

For Toppings:

- Okonomiyaki sauce
- Japanese mayonnaise
- Bonito flakes (katsuobushi)
- Aonori (seaweed flakes)
- Chopped green onions

Instructions:

Making the Batter:

In a large mixing bowl, combine all-purpose flour, dashi, and eggs. Whisk until smooth.
Add thinly shredded cabbage, chopped green onions, tenkasu or tempura flakes, and cooked squid or shrimp (if using) to the batter. Mix well to coat the ingredients evenly.
Season the batter with salt and pepper to taste.

Cooking Okonomiyaki:

Heat a griddle or large non-stick skillet over medium heat.

Pour a ladle of the batter onto the griddle, forming a round pancake about 1/2 to 1 inch thick.

Cook the okonomiyaki for 5-7 minutes on each side or until both sides are golden brown and the center is cooked through.

Flip the okonomiyaki using two spatulas to ensure it holds together.

Toppings and Serving:

Transfer the cooked okonomiyaki to a plate.

Drizzle okonomiyaki sauce and Japanese mayonnaise over the top.

Sprinkle bonito flakes (katsuobushi), aonori (seaweed flakes), and chopped green onions as desired.

Serve the Japanese Okonomiyaki hot.

Cut it into wedges and enjoy this delicious and savory vegetable pancake!

Note: Okonomiyaki is a versatile dish, and you can customize the ingredients and toppings according to your preferences. Common variations include adding yakisoba noodles or cheese for added flavor.

Rice and Noodle Dishes:

Chicken Fried Rice

Ingredients:

For the Rice:

- 2 cups cooked jasmine rice (preferably chilled or leftover)
- 2 tablespoons vegetable oil
- 2 eggs, lightly beaten
- Salt and pepper to taste

For the Chicken:

- 1 lb (about 450g) boneless, skinless chicken breasts, diced
- 2 tablespoons soy sauce
- 1 tablespoon oyster sauce
- 1 tablespoon cornstarch
- 1 teaspoon sesame oil
- 1/2 teaspoon black pepper
- 2 tablespoons vegetable oil for cooking

For the Vegetables:

- 1 cup frozen peas and carrots, thawed
- 1/2 cup corn kernels (fresh or frozen)
- 1/2 cup diced bell peppers
- 4 green onions, sliced

For Stir-Frying:

- 2 cloves garlic, minced
- 1 teaspoon fresh ginger, grated
- 2 tablespoons soy sauce
- 1 tablespoon oyster sauce
- 1 tablespoon hoisin sauce

For Garnish:

- Sliced green onions
- Sesame seeds

Instructions:

Cooking the Chicken:

> In a bowl, combine diced chicken with soy sauce, oyster sauce, cornstarch, sesame oil, and black pepper. Mix well and let it marinate for about 15-20 minutes.
> Heat 2 tablespoons of vegetable oil in a wok or large skillet over medium-high heat.
> Add the marinated chicken to the wok and stir-fry until it's fully cooked and has a golden brown exterior. Remove the chicken from the wok and set it aside.

Making the Rice:

> Heat 2 tablespoons of vegetable oil in the same wok over medium heat.
> Add the lightly beaten eggs, season with salt and pepper, and scramble them until they are cooked through. Remove the scrambled eggs from the wok and set them aside.
> Add the cooked jasmine rice to the wok. Break up any clumps and stir-fry the rice until it's heated through and slightly crispy.

Stir-Frying:

> Push the rice to the side of the wok. Add a bit more oil if needed.
> Add minced garlic and grated ginger to the wok. Stir-fry for about 30 seconds until fragrant.
> Add thawed peas and carrots, corn kernels, diced bell peppers, and sliced green onions to the wok. Stir-fry for 2-3 minutes until the vegetables are crisp-tender.
> Return the cooked chicken and scrambled eggs to the wok.
> Pour soy sauce, oyster sauce, and hoisin sauce over the ingredients. Toss everything together until well-combined.

Serving:

    Serve Chicken Fried Rice hot.
    Garnish with sliced green onions and sesame seeds.
    Enjoy this classic and delicious Chicken Fried Rice!

Note: Feel free to customize the vegetables and adjust the seasonings according to your taste preferences. Using chilled or leftover rice helps achieve the best texture in fried rice.

Pad See Ew (Thai Stir-Fried Noodles)

Ingredients:

For the Sauce:

- 3 tablespoons soy sauce
- 1 tablespoon oyster sauce
- 1 tablespoon fish sauce
- 1 tablespoon sugar
- 1 teaspoon dark soy sauce (optional, for color)

For the Stir-Fried Noodles:

- 8 oz (about 225g) wide rice noodles
- 2 tablespoons vegetable oil
- 2 cloves garlic, minced
- 1 cup Chinese broccoli or broccoli florets
- 1 cup sliced chicken, beef, or tofu
- 2 eggs, lightly beaten
- White pepper to taste
- Crushed peanuts for garnish (optional)
- Lime wedges for serving

Instructions:

Preparing the Sauce:

In a bowl, whisk together soy sauce, oyster sauce, fish sauce, sugar, and dark soy sauce (if using). Set aside.

Cooking the Rice Noodles:

Cook the wide rice noodles according to the package instructions. Drain and set aside.

Stir-Frying:

Heat vegetable oil in a wok or large skillet over medium-high heat.
Add minced garlic to the wok and stir-fry for about 30 seconds until fragrant.
Add sliced chicken, beef, or tofu to the wok. Cook until the protein is fully cooked.
Push the cooked protein to one side of the wok. Pour the lightly beaten eggs into the other side and scramble until they are almost fully cooked.
Add Chinese broccoli or broccoli florets to the wok. Stir everything together.
Add the cooked rice noodles to the wok.
Pour the prepared sauce over the noodles. Toss everything together until the noodles are well-coated and heated through.
Season with white pepper to taste.

Serving:

Serve Pad See Ew hot.
Garnish with crushed peanuts if desired.
Serve with lime wedges on the side for squeezing over the noodles.
Enjoy this classic Thai stir-fried noodle dish!

Note: Adjust the level of sweetness or saltiness by varying the amount of sugar or fish sauce. You can customize the protein and vegetables according to your preferences. The dark soy sauce is optional and primarily used for color; it can be omitted if not available.

Pineapple Fried Rice

Ingredients:

For the Pineapple Fried Rice:

- 2 cups cooked jasmine rice (preferably chilled or leftover)
- 2 tablespoons vegetable oil
- 1 cup diced pineapple (fresh or canned)
- 1 cup diced cooked chicken or shrimp
- 1/2 cup diced ham
- 1/2 cup peas (fresh or frozen)
- 1/2 cup diced bell peppers (mix of colors)
- 2 eggs, lightly beaten
- 3 green onions, sliced
- 1/4 cup cashews or peanuts (optional)
- Lime wedges for serving

For the Sauce:

- 3 tablespoons soy sauce
- 1 tablespoon fish sauce
- 1 tablespoon oyster sauce
- 1 tablespoon brown sugar
- 1 teaspoon curry powder (optional, for flavor)

Instructions:

Making the Sauce:

> In a small bowl, whisk together soy sauce, fish sauce, oyster sauce, brown sugar, and curry powder (if using). Set aside.

Stir-Frying:

> Heat vegetable oil in a wok or large skillet over medium-high heat.
> Add diced chicken or shrimp to the wok and stir-fry until fully cooked.
> Push the cooked protein to one side of the wok. Pour the lightly beaten eggs into the other side and scramble until they are almost fully cooked.
> Add diced ham, peas, and diced bell peppers to the wok. Stir everything together.

Add diced pineapple to the wok and stir-fry for an additional 1-2 minutes.

Combining with Rice:

Add the cooked jasmine rice to the wok. Break up any clumps and stir-fry until the rice is heated through.
Pour the prepared sauce over the rice and toss everything together until well-coated.
Add sliced green onions to the wok and toss again.

Serving:

Serve Pineapple Fried Rice hot.
Garnish with cashews or peanuts if desired.
Serve with lime wedges on the side for squeezing over the rice.
Enjoy this flavorful and tropical-inspired fried rice!

Note: Feel free to customize the protein and vegetables based on your preferences. Adjust the level of sweetness or saltiness by varying the amount of brown sugar or soy sauce. The curry powder adds an extra layer of flavor, but you can omit it if you prefer a more traditional fried rice taste.

Bibimbap (Korean Mixed Rice)

Ingredients:

For the Bibimbap Rice:

- 2 cups cooked short-grain rice (preferably Korean or sushi rice)
- 2 tablespoons sesame oil

For the Vegetables:

- 1 cup julienned carrots, sautéed
- 1 cup sliced shiitake mushrooms, sautéed
- 1 cup spinach, blanched and seasoned with sesame oil and salt
- 1 cup mung bean sprouts, blanched and seasoned with soy sauce and sesame oil

For the Protein:

1 cup sliced beef (ribeye or sirloin), marinated and stir-fried

- *Marinade:*
    - 2 tablespoons soy sauce
    - 1 tablespoon sugar
    - 1 tablespoon mirin
    - 1 tablespoon sesame oil
    - 2 cloves garlic, minced

For the Bibimbap Sauce (Gochujang Sauce):

- 2 tablespoons gochujang (Korean red pepper paste)
- 1 tablespoon soy sauce
- 1 tablespoon sesame oil
- 1 tablespoon sugar
- 1 tablespoon water

For Garnish:

- Fried egg (sunny-side-up or over easy)
- Sesame seeds
- Sliced green onions

Instructions:

Preparing the Vegetables:

Julienne the carrots and sauté in a pan with a bit of oil until they are tender. Set aside.
Slice the shiitake mushrooms and sauté until they are cooked. Set aside.
Blanch the spinach in boiling water for a minute, then rinse with cold water. Season with a bit of sesame oil and salt. Set aside.
Blanch the mung bean sprouts in boiling water for a minute, then season with soy sauce and sesame oil. Set aside.

Marinating and Cooking the Beef:

Mix the ingredients for the marinade in a bowl.
Slice the beef thinly and marinate for about 20-30 minutes.
Stir-fry the marinated beef in a hot pan until fully cooked. Set aside.

Making the Gochujang Sauce:

In a small bowl, whisk together gochujang, soy sauce, sesame oil, sugar, and water. Set aside.

Assembling Bibimbap:

Place a serving of cooked rice in the center of a bowl.
Arrange the sautéed vegetables and cooked beef on top of the rice in separate sections.
Add the fried egg on top.
Garnish with sesame seeds and sliced green onions.
Serve Bibimbap with the Gochujang Sauce on the side.
Mix everything together just before eating to enjoy the flavorful combination.

Note: You can customize the vegetables and protein based on your preferences. Bibimbap is highly adaptable, and you can use different ingredients according to your taste. Adjust the level of spiciness in the Gochujang Sauce to your liking.

Hainanese Chicken Rice

Ingredients:

For the Chicken:

- 1 whole chicken (about 3-4 lbs)
- 4 slices ginger
- 3 stalks green onions, cut into sections
- Salt for rubbing the chicken

For the Rice:

- 2 cups jasmine rice
- 4 cups chicken broth (from cooking the chicken)
- 4 slices ginger
- 2 cloves garlic, minced
- 1 tablespoon sesame oil

For the Chicken Sauce:

- 2 tablespoons light soy sauce
- 1 tablespoon oyster sauce
- 1 tablespoon chicken broth (from cooking the chicken)
- 1 tablespoon sesame oil
- 1 teaspoon sugar
- 1/4 teaspoon white pepper

For the Dipping Sauce:

- Soy sauce with minced ginger

For Garnish:

- Fresh cilantro leaves
- Sliced cucumber

Instructions:

Cooking the Chicken:

Rinse the chicken thoroughly, inside and out. Pat it dry with paper towels.
Rub salt over the chicken skin and inside the cavity. This helps to remove impurities and gives the chicken a smooth texture.
Stuff the chicken cavity with ginger slices and green onion sections.
Bring a large pot of water to a boil. Carefully lower the whole chicken into the boiling water, breast-side down. Reduce heat to low, cover, and simmer for about 40-50 minutes or until the chicken is cooked through.
Remove the chicken from the pot and immediately plunge it into a bowl of ice water to stop the cooking process. Let it cool completely.

Cooking the Rice:

Rinse the jasmine rice under cold water until the water runs clear.
In a saucepan, heat sesame oil over medium heat. Add minced garlic and ginger slices. Sauté for about 1-2 minutes until fragrant.
Add the rinsed rice to the saucepan and stir to coat it with the aromatic mixture.
Transfer the rice to a rice cooker. Add chicken broth (from cooking the chicken) and cook the rice according to the rice cooker instructions.

Preparing the Chicken Sauce:

In a bowl, combine light soy sauce, oyster sauce, chicken broth, sesame oil, sugar, and white pepper. Mix well to create the chicken sauce.

Assembling Hainanese Chicken Rice:

Slice the cooked chicken into bite-sized pieces.
Arrange the chicken slices on a serving plate. Garnish with fresh cilantro leaves and sliced cucumber.
Serve the chicken with the cooked jasmine rice on the side.
Drizzle the chicken sauce over the chicken slices.
Prepare a dipping sauce using soy sauce and minced ginger.

Enjoy this classic Hainanese Chicken Rice with the flavorful chicken sauce and fragrant jasmine rice!

Note: You can use the remaining chicken broth as a soup base or freeze it for future use. The ice water bath is crucial to achieving tender and smooth chicken skin. Adjust the seasonings in the chicken sauce according to your taste preference.

Curries:

Thai Green Curry with Chicken

Ingredients:

For the Green Curry Paste:

- 2 green Thai bird chilies, chopped (adjust to taste for spiciness)
- 2 stalks lemongrass, sliced (only use the bottom half)
- 3 shallots, chopped
- 4 cloves garlic, minced
- 1 thumb-sized piece of galangal or ginger, sliced
- 1 teaspoon ground coriander
- 1/2 teaspoon ground cumin
- Zest of 1 lime
- 1 bunch fresh cilantro, stems included
- 2 kaffir lime leaves, stems removed
- 1 tablespoon fish sauce

For the Green Curry:

- 1 lb (about 450g) boneless, skinless chicken breasts or thighs, sliced
- 2 tablespoons vegetable oil
- 1 can (14 oz) coconut milk
- 1 cup chicken broth
- 1 tablespoon green curry paste (from above)
- 1 cup Thai eggplants, halved (or substitute with regular eggplants)
- 1 red bell pepper, sliced
- 1 cup bamboo shoots, sliced
- 1 tablespoon fish sauce (adjust to taste)
- 1 tablespoon sugar
- Fresh basil leaves for garnish
- Cooked jasmine rice for serving

Instructions:

Making the Green Curry Paste:

In a food processor, combine green Thai bird chilies, lemongrass, shallots, garlic, galangal or ginger, ground coriander, ground cumin, lime zest, cilantro, kaffir lime leaves, and fish sauce.

Process the ingredients until a smooth paste is formed. You may need to scrape down the sides of the food processor to ensure all the ingredients are well-blended.

Cooking the Green Curry:

Heat vegetable oil in a large pot or wok over medium heat.
Add 1 tablespoon of the green curry paste to the pot and sauté for about 1-2 minutes until fragrant.
Add the sliced chicken to the pot and cook until it's no longer pink.
Pour in coconut milk and chicken broth. Stir in the remaining green curry paste.
Add Thai eggplants, red bell pepper, and bamboo shoots to the pot. Simmer for about 15-20 minutes until the vegetables are tender.
Season the curry with fish sauce and sugar. Adjust the seasonings to taste.

Serving:

Serve the Thai Green Curry hot over cooked jasmine rice.
Garnish with fresh basil leaves.
Enjoy this aromatic and flavorful Thai Green Curry with Chicken!

Note: You can customize the vegetables in the curry based on your preferences. Adjust the amount of green Thai bird chilies in the curry paste to control the level of spiciness.

Japanese Curry Rice

Ingredients:

For the Curry Roux:

- 3 tablespoons vegetable oil
- 1 onion, finely chopped
- 2 carrots, peeled and diced
- 2 potatoes, peeled and diced
- 2 cloves garlic, minced
- 1 pound (about 450g) meat of your choice (beef, chicken, or pork), diced
- 3 tablespoons curry powder
- 3 tablespoons all-purpose flour
- 4 cups chicken or beef broth
- 2 tablespoons soy sauce
- 1 tablespoon Worcestershire sauce
- 1 tablespoon ketchup
- Salt and pepper to taste

For Serving:

- Cooked Japanese short-grain rice

Instructions:

Preparing the Curry Roux:

In a large pot or Dutch oven, heat vegetable oil over medium heat.
Add finely chopped onions and minced garlic. Sauté until the onions are translucent.
Add diced meat to the pot and cook until browned.
Stir in diced carrots and potatoes. Cook for a few minutes until they begin to soften.
Sprinkle curry powder and flour over the vegetables and meat. Mix well to coat everything evenly.
Gradually pour in chicken or beef broth, stirring constantly to avoid lumps.
Add soy sauce, Worcestershire sauce, and ketchup to the pot. Mix well.
Season with salt and pepper to taste.

Simmer the curry over low heat for about 30-45 minutes, or until the vegetables are tender and the curry has thickened.

Serving:

Serve the Japanese Curry over a bed of cooked Japanese short-grain rice. Enjoy the delicious Japanese Curry Rice!

Note: You can customize the vegetables and meat based on your preferences. Adjust the thickness of the curry by adding more or less broth. Japanese Curry is often served with fukujinzuke (pickles) or rakkyo (Japanese scallions) on the side for added flavor.

Indian Vegetable Curry

Ingredients:

For the Curry Base:

- 2 tablespoons vegetable oil
- 1 large onion, finely chopped
- 2 cloves garlic, minced
- 1 tablespoon ginger, grated
- 1 large tomato, chopped
- 1 cup tomato puree
- 1 teaspoon ground turmeric
- 1 teaspoon ground cumin
- 1 teaspoon ground coriander
- 1/2 teaspoon chili powder (adjust to taste)
- 1/2 teaspoon garam masala
- Salt to taste

For the Vegetables:

- 2 cups mixed vegetables (potatoes, carrots, peas, cauliflower, bell peppers, etc.), chopped
- 1 cup spinach or kale, chopped
- 1 can (14 oz) chickpeas, drained and rinsed (optional)

For Finishing:

- 1/2 cup coconut milk or heavy cream
- Fresh cilantro, chopped, for garnish
- Lemon wedges for serving

Instructions:

Making the Curry Base:

Heat vegetable oil in a large pan or Dutch oven over medium heat.

Add finely chopped onions and sauté until they become translucent.
Add minced garlic and grated ginger. Sauté for an additional minute until fragrant.
Add chopped tomatoes and cook until they break down and form a thick paste.
Stir in tomato puree, ground turmeric, ground cumin, ground coriander, chili powder, garam masala, and salt. Mix well.
Cook the spice mixture for 2-3 minutes until the oil begins to separate.

Cooking the Vegetables:

Add the mixed vegetables to the pan. Stir well to coat them with the spice mixture.
Pour in enough water to cover the vegetables. Bring the mixture to a simmer and cook until the vegetables are tender.
Add chopped spinach or kale and chickpeas (if using). Cook for an additional 3-5 minutes.

Finishing the Curry:

Pour in coconut milk or heavy cream. Stir well and let it simmer for another 5 minutes.
Adjust the seasoning if needed. If you prefer a thicker curry, let it simmer a bit longer.

Serving:

Serve the Indian Vegetable Curry over rice or with naan bread.
Garnish with chopped cilantro.
Serve with lemon wedges on the side for squeezing over the curry.
Enjoy this flavorful and hearty Indian Vegetable Curry!

Note: Feel free to customize the vegetables based on your preferences. Adjust the spice levels to suit your taste. You can also add protein sources like paneer or tofu for extra richness.

Panang Curry with Beef

Ingredients:

For the Panang Curry Paste:

- 2 tablespoons roasted peanuts
- 2 tablespoons red curry paste
- 1 teaspoon ground coriander
- 1/2 teaspoon ground cumin
- 2 tablespoons fish sauce
- 1 tablespoon soy sauce
- 1 tablespoon brown sugar
- 1 tablespoon minced lemongrass
- 2 cloves garlic, minced
- 1 teaspoon grated ginger
- 2 kaffir lime leaves, finely chopped (optional)
- 1 teaspoon shrimp paste (optional)

For the Curry:

- 1 lb (about 450g) beef sirloin or flank, thinly sliced
- 2 tablespoons vegetable oil
- 1 can (14 oz) coconut milk
- 1 cup chicken or beef broth
- 2 tablespoons Panang curry paste (from above)
- 1 tablespoon brown sugar
- 1 tablespoon fish sauce
- 1 tablespoon lime juice
- 1 red bell pepper, thinly sliced
- 1/2 cup Thai basil leaves, for garnish
- Cooked jasmine rice for serving

Instructions:

Making the Panang Curry Paste:

In a blender or food processor, combine roasted peanuts, red curry paste, ground coriander, ground cumin, fish sauce, soy sauce, brown sugar, minced lemongrass, minced garlic, grated ginger, kaffir lime leaves (if using), and shrimp paste (if using).

Blend the ingredients until you get a smooth paste. Set aside.

Cooking the Curry:

Heat vegetable oil in a large pan or wok over medium heat.
Add 2 tablespoons of the Panang curry paste to the pan. Stir-fry for about 1-2 minutes until fragrant.
Add thinly sliced beef to the pan and cook until browned on all sides.
Pour in coconut milk and chicken or beef broth. Stir in brown sugar, fish sauce, and lime juice.
Bring the mixture to a simmer and cook for about 15-20 minutes until the beef is cooked through and the flavors meld together.
Add thinly sliced red bell pepper to the pan and cook for an additional 3-5 minutes until the peppers are tender.

Serving:

Serve Panang Curry with Beef hot over cooked jasmine rice.
Garnish with Thai basil leaves.
Enjoy the rich and flavorful Panang Curry with Beef!

Note: Adjust the amount of Panang curry paste based on your spice preference. You can find kaffir lime leaves and shrimp paste in Asian grocery stores. Customize the vegetables according to your liking.

Malaysian Rendang Curry

Ingredients:

For the Rendang Paste:

- 8 dried red chilies, soaked in hot water and deseeded
- 1 large onion, roughly chopped
- 4 cloves garlic
- 1 thumb-sized piece of galangal or ginger, sliced
- 2 lemongrass stalks, sliced (only use the bottom half)
- 1 teaspoon ground turmeric
- 1 teaspoon ground coriander
- 1 teaspoon ground cumin
- 1/2 teaspoon ground cinnamon
- 1/2 teaspoon ground nutmeg
- 1/2 teaspoon ground cloves
- 1/2 teaspoon black peppercorns
- 4 tablespoons vegetable oil

For the Rendang Curry:

- 2 lbs (about 900g) beef, cut into chunks (beef brisket or chuck works well)
- 2 cans (28 oz each) coconut milk
- 4 kaffir lime leaves, torn
- 2 turmeric leaves, torn (optional)
- Salt to taste
- Sugar to taste
- Desiccated coconut for garnish (optional)
- Toasted coconut for garnish (optional)
- Lime wedges for serving
- Cooked jasmine rice for serving

Instructions:

Making the Rendang Paste:

> In a blender or food processor, combine soaked and deseeded dried red chilies, chopped onion, garlic, sliced galangal or ginger, sliced lemongrass, ground

turmeric, ground coriander, ground cumin, ground cinnamon, ground nutmeg, ground cloves, and black peppercorns.

Blend the ingredients until you get a smooth paste. Add a bit of water if needed. Heat vegetable oil in a large pot over medium heat. Add the rendang paste and sauté for about 5-7 minutes until fragrant.

Cooking the Rendang Curry:

Add the beef chunks to the pot and cook until they are browned on all sides.
Pour in the coconut milk and bring the mixture to a boil.
Add torn kaffir lime leaves and turmeric leaves (if using) to the pot. Reduce the heat to low and let it simmer.
Allow the curry to simmer for 2-3 hours, stirring occasionally, until the beef is tender and the curry has thickened.
Season the rendang curry with salt and sugar to taste. Adjust the seasoning according to your preference.
Continue to simmer until the rendang reaches a rich and dark color, and the oil starts to separate.

Serving:

Serve Malaysian Rendang Curry hot over cooked jasmine rice.
Garnish with desiccated coconut or toasted coconut if desired.
Serve with lime wedges on the side for squeezing over the curry.
Enjoy the rich and aromatic Malaysian Rendang Curry!

Note: Turmeric leaves add a distinct fragrance to the rendang, but if unavailable, the dish is still delicious without them. Adjust the level of spiciness by varying the amount of dried red chilies.

Dim Sum:

Har Gow (Shrimp Dumplings)

Ingredients:

For the Dough:

- 1 cup wheat starch
- 1/4 cup tapioca starch
- 1/4 teaspoon salt
- 1 cup boiling water
- 1 tablespoon vegetable oil

For the Shrimp Filling:

- 1/2 lb (about 225g) raw shrimp, peeled, deveined, and finely chopped
- 1/4 cup bamboo shoots, finely chopped
- 1/4 cup water chestnuts, finely chopped
- 1 tablespoon cornstarch
- 1 tablespoon soy sauce
- 1 teaspoon sugar
- 1 teaspoon sesame oil
- 1/2 teaspoon white pepper
- 1 green onion, finely chopped

For Wrapping:

- Round dumpling wrappers (har gow wrappers)
- Cornstarch for dusting

Instructions:

Making the Dough:

In a mixing bowl, combine wheat starch, tapioca starch, and salt.

Gradually add boiling water while stirring continuously to form a dough.
Knead the dough until it's smooth and elastic.
Add vegetable oil and knead again until well incorporated.
Cover the dough and let it rest for 20-30 minutes.

Preparing the Shrimp Filling:

In a bowl, combine chopped shrimp, bamboo shoots, water chestnuts, cornstarch, soy sauce, sugar, sesame oil, white pepper, and chopped green onion.
Mix well until the ingredients are evenly distributed.

Forming the Har Gow:

Roll the rested dough into a long cylinder shape and divide it into small portions.
Take a portion of the dough and roll it into a ball.
Flatten the dough ball into a round wrapper, ensuring the edges are thinner than the center.
Place a spoonful of shrimp filling in the center of the wrapper.
Pleat and seal the edges to form a half-moon shape. Ensure the dumpling is well-sealed.
Repeat the process until all the dough and filling are used.

Steaming the Har Gow:

Line a steamer basket with parchment paper or cabbage leaves to prevent sticking.
Place the har gow in the steamer basket, leaving space between each dumpling.
Steam over high heat for 8-10 minutes or until the wrappers become translucent and the shrimp filling is cooked through.
Serve the har gow immediately with soy sauce or your favorite dipping sauce.
Enjoy these delicious and delicate shrimp dumplings!

Note: Har Gow is best enjoyed fresh out of the steamer. Ensure the dumplings are well-sealed to prevent leakage during steaming. Adjust the seasoning of the shrimp filling according to your taste preferences.

Siu Mai (Pork and Shrimp Dumplings)

Ingredients:

For the Filling:

- 1/2 lb ground pork
- 1/2 lb shrimp, peeled, deveined, and finely chopped
- 1/4 cup water chestnuts, finely chopped
- 2 tablespoons green onions, finely chopped
- 1 tablespoon soy sauce
- 1 tablespoon oyster sauce
- 1 tablespoon sesame oil
- 1 tablespoon cornstarch
- 1 teaspoon sugar
- 1/2 teaspoon white pepper
- Wonton wrappers (round or square)
- Peas or carrot slices for garnish (optional)

Instructions:

Preparing the Filling:

In a bowl, combine ground pork, finely chopped shrimp, water chestnuts, green onions, soy sauce, oyster sauce, sesame oil, cornstarch, sugar, and white pepper. Mix the ingredients well until evenly combined.

Assembling the Siu Mai:

If using square wonton wrappers, cut them into circles using a round cutter or a glass.
Place a small spoonful of the filling in the center of each wrapper.
Gather the edges of the wrapper, leaving the filling exposed at the top. Press the edges together to form a basket shape.
Place a pea or a slice of carrot on top for garnish, pressing it gently into the filling.

Steaming the Siu Mai:

Line a steamer basket with parchment paper or cabbage leaves to prevent sticking.
Arrange the siu mai in the steamer basket, leaving space between each dumpling.
Steam over high heat for 10-12 minutes or until the pork is cooked through and the wrappers are translucent.
Serve the siu mai immediately with soy sauce or your favorite dipping sauce.
Enjoy these flavorful and delicate pork and shrimp dumplings!

Note: Siu Mai can be customized with additional ingredients like mushrooms or bamboo shoots. Ensure the wrappers are well-sealed to prevent the filling from falling out during steaming. Experiment with different shapes for a creative presentation.

Char Siu Bao (BBQ Pork Buns)

Ingredients:

For the Char Siu Filling:

- 1 cup char siu (Chinese BBQ pork), finely chopped
- 2 tablespoons hoisin sauce
- 1 tablespoon soy sauce
- 1 tablespoon oyster sauce
- 1 tablespoon sugar
- 1 tablespoon cornstarch
- 1/4 cup water

For the Dough:

- 2 1/2 cups all-purpose flour
- 1/4 cup sugar
- 1 tablespoon baking powder
- 1 tablespoon vegetable oil
- 1 cup warm water

For Assembling and Steaming:

- Cornstarch for dusting
- 12 parchment paper squares (about 3x3 inches)
- Bamboo steamer or steaming rack

Instructions:

Preparing the Char Siu Filling:

In a saucepan, combine chopped char siu, hoisin sauce, soy sauce, oyster sauce, sugar, cornstarch, and water.
Cook over medium heat, stirring continuously, until the mixture thickens and becomes a cohesive filling. Set aside to cool.

Making the Dough:

In a large mixing bowl, combine all-purpose flour, sugar, and baking powder.

Add vegetable oil to warm water and gradually pour it into the dry ingredients, stirring continuously.

Knead the dough until it becomes smooth and elastic. Cover and let it rest for about 15-20 minutes.

Assembling the Char Siu Bao:

Roll out the dough on a floured surface into a long log shape.
Divide the dough into 12 equal portions.
Roll each portion into a ball and then flatten it into a small disc, ensuring the edges are thinner than the center.
Place a spoonful of the cooled char siu filling in the center of each dough disc.
Gather the edges of the dough, pleating and twisting to seal the bun at the top.
Pinch the edges together to secure the filling.
Place each bun on a parchment paper square dusted with cornstarch.

Steaming the Char Siu Bao:

Heat water in a steamer over high heat.
Place the buns in a bamboo steamer or on a steaming rack, leaving space between each bun.
Steam over high heat for 15-20 minutes or until the buns are cooked through and fluffy.
Serve the Char Siu Bao hot, and enjoy the delicious BBQ pork-filled buns!

Note: You can adjust the sweetness and saltiness of the filling by varying the amount of sugar and soy sauce. Ensure the dough is rested to achieve a soft and fluffy texture. Store any leftover buns in an airtight container in the refrigerator and reheat before serving.

Egg Custard Tarts

Ingredients:

For the Pastry:

- 1 1/4 cups all-purpose flour
- 1/4 cup powdered sugar
- 1/2 cup unsalted butter, cold and cut into small cubes
- 1 egg yolk
- 1-2 tablespoons ice water

For the Custard Filling:

- 1 cup whole milk
- 1/2 cup heavy cream
- 1/2 cup granulated sugar
- 4 large eggs
- 1 teaspoon vanilla extract
- Pinch of salt

Instructions:

Making the Pastry:

In a food processor, combine all-purpose flour and powdered sugar. Pulse to mix.
Add cold, cubed butter to the flour mixture and pulse until the mixture resembles coarse crumbs.
Add the egg yolk and pulse a few times.
Gradually add ice water, one tablespoon at a time, pulsing until the dough comes together.
Turn the dough out onto a floured surface, knead it into a ball, flatten it into a disc, and wrap it in plastic wrap.
Refrigerate the dough for at least 30 minutes.

Pre-baking the Pastry:

Preheat your oven to 375°F (190°C).

Roll out the chilled dough on a floured surface to about 1/8 inch thickness.

Cut out circles of dough using a round cookie cutter or a glass that fits the size of your tart molds.

Gently press the dough circles into greased tart molds, trimming any excess dough.

Prick the bottom of the pastry with a fork.

Line the tart shells with parchment paper and fill them with pie weights or dried beans.

Blind bake the pastry for about 12-15 minutes or until the edges are lightly golden. Remove the weights and parchment paper and bake for an additional 5 minutes until the bottom is cooked.

Allow the tart shells to cool while preparing the custard filling.

Making the Custard Filling:

In a saucepan, heat whole milk and heavy cream over medium heat until it just starts to simmer. Remove from heat.

In a bowl, whisk together granulated sugar, eggs, vanilla extract, and a pinch of salt.

Slowly pour the warm milk mixture into the egg mixture, whisking continuously to avoid curdling.

Strain the custard mixture through a fine mesh sieve to ensure a smooth texture.

Baking the Egg Custard Tarts:

Preheat your oven to 350°F (175°C).

Pour the custard mixture into the pre-baked tart shells.

Bake the tarts for 20-25 minutes or until the custard is set and slightly golden on top.

Allow the tarts to cool before removing them from the molds.

Serve the Egg Custard Tarts at room temperature and enjoy!

Note: You can use store-bought tart shells to save time. Adjust the sugar in the custard filling according to your sweetness preference. These tarts are best enjoyed on the day they are made.

Xiao Long Bao (Soup Dumplings)

Ingredients:

For the Filling:

- 1/2 lb ground pork
- 1/4 cup chicken or pork stock
- 2 tablespoons soy sauce
- 1 tablespoon sesame oil
- 1 tablespoon Shaoxing wine (Chinese rice wine)
- 1 teaspoon sugar
- 1 teaspoon grated ginger
- 1/2 cup finely chopped green onions
- 1/2 cup finely chopped napa cabbage (blanched and squeezed to remove excess water)
- Gelatin cubes made from 1/2 cup rich pork or chicken stock, chilled (for the soup filling)

For the Dumpling Dough:

- 2 cups all-purpose flour
- 3/4 cup warm water
- 1/2 teaspoon salt
- Cornstarch for dusting

Instructions:

Making the Filling:

In a bowl, combine ground pork, chicken or pork stock, soy sauce, sesame oil, Shaoxing wine, sugar, grated ginger, chopped green onions, and blanched napa cabbage.
Mix the ingredients thoroughly until well combined. Refrigerate the filling while preparing the dough.
Cut the chilled gelatin cubes into small pieces. Place a small piece of gelatin in the center of each dumpling filling.

Making the Dumpling Dough:

In a large bowl, combine all-purpose flour, warm water, and salt.
Knead the mixture until a smooth and elastic dough forms.
Cover the dough and let it rest for about 30 minutes.

Assembling the Xiao Long Bao:

Roll out the dough into a long cylinder shape and cut it into small portions.
Roll each portion into a ball and then flatten it into a small disc.
Dust the working surface with cornstarch and roll each disc into a thin wrapper, ensuring the edges are thinner than the center.
Place a spoonful of the filling in the center of each wrapper, ensuring there is a gelatin cube in the middle.
Pleat and seal the edges, ensuring the dumpling is well-sealed to prevent leakage during steaming.

Steaming the Xiao Long Bao:

Line a steamer basket with parchment paper or cabbage leaves to prevent sticking.
Arrange the Xiao Long Bao in the steamer basket, leaving space between each dumpling.
Steam over high heat for 10-12 minutes or until the dumplings are cooked through and the wrappers are translucent.
Serve the Xiao Long Bao hot with a dipping sauce made from soy sauce, vinegar, and ginger.
Carefully enjoy these delicate and flavorful soup dumplings!

Note: Xiao Long Bao requires practice to master the pleating technique. Ensure the wrappers are thin to allow the soup to be released when bitten. Adjust the filling ingredients according to your taste preferences.

Street Food:

Pad Thai

Ingredients:

For the Pad Thai Sauce:

- 3 tablespoons tamarind paste
- 3 tablespoons fish sauce
- 1 tablespoon soy sauce
- 1 tablespoon oyster sauce
- 1 tablespoon sugar
- 1/2 teaspoon chili flakes (adjust to taste)
- 1/4 cup chicken broth or water

For the Pad Thai:

- 8 oz (about 225g) flat rice noodles, soaked in warm water until softened
- 2 tablespoons vegetable oil
- 1 cup firm tofu, cubed
- 2 cloves garlic, minced
- 1 cup shrimp, peeled and deveined (optional)
- 2 eggs, lightly beaten
- 2 cups bean sprouts
- 1 cup Chinese chives or green onions, cut into 2-inch pieces
- 1/4 cup crushed peanuts
- Lime wedges for serving

Instructions:

Making the Pad Thai Sauce:

In a bowl, whisk together tamarind paste, fish sauce, soy sauce, oyster sauce, sugar, chili flakes, and chicken broth or water. Set aside.

Preparing the Pad Thai:

Heat vegetable oil in a wok or large skillet over medium-high heat.

Add cubed tofu and cook until golden brown. If using shrimp, add them and cook until pink and opaque.

Push the tofu and shrimp to one side of the wok. Add minced garlic to the other side and sauté until fragrant.

Push everything to one side again and pour the beaten eggs into the wok. Scramble the eggs until cooked.

Add the soaked rice noodles to the wok and pour the prepared Pad Thai sauce over them.

Toss everything together until the noodles are well-coated in the sauce and heated through.

Add bean sprouts and Chinese chives or green onions to the wok. Toss for an additional 1-2 minutes until the vegetables are slightly cooked but still crisp.

Taste and adjust the seasoning if needed.

Serving:

Serve Pad Thai hot, garnished with crushed peanuts and lime wedges on the side.

Enjoy this classic Thai noodle dish!

Note: Customize Pad Thai by adding other protein sources like chicken or beef. Adjust the level of spiciness by varying the amount of chili flakes. You can also add extra lime juice, fish sauce, or sugar according to your taste preferences.

Banh Mi (Vietnamese Sandwich)

Ingredients:

For the Marinade (for protein of choice):

- 1 lb (about 450g) protein of choice (chicken, pork, or tofu)
- 3 tablespoons soy sauce
- 2 tablespoons fish sauce
- 2 tablespoons honey or sugar
- 1 tablespoon vegetable oil
- 2 cloves garlic, minced
- 1 teaspoon five-spice powder (optional)

For the Sriracha Mayonnaise:

- 1/2 cup mayonnaise
- 2 tablespoons Sriracha sauce (adjust to taste)

For the Pickled Vegetables:

- 1 cup julienned carrots
- 1 cup julienned daikon radish
- 1/2 cup rice vinegar
- 1/4 cup sugar
- 1 teaspoon salt

For Assembling the Banh Mi:

- Baguettes or Vietnamese-style rolls
- Fresh cilantro leaves
- Fresh jalapeño slices
- Sliced cucumber
- Maggi sauce or soy sauce for drizzling

Instructions:

Marinating the Protein:

In a bowl, combine soy sauce, fish sauce, honey or sugar, vegetable oil, minced garlic, and five-spice powder.

Add the protein (chicken, pork, or tofu) to the marinade and let it marinate for at least 30 minutes, preferably longer.

Cook the marinated protein by grilling, baking, or pan-frying until fully cooked and slightly caramelized.

Making the Sriracha Mayonnaise:

In a small bowl, mix mayonnaise and Sriracha sauce until well combined. Adjust the Sriracha to your desired level of spiciness.

Pickling the Vegetables:

In a bowl, combine julienned carrots and daikon radish.

In a separate bowl, mix rice vinegar, sugar, and salt until the sugar and salt dissolve.

Pour the vinegar mixture over the vegetables and let them marinate for at least 30 minutes.

Assembling the Banh Mi:

Cut the baguettes or Vietnamese-style rolls in half lengthwise.

Spread a generous amount of Sriracha mayonnaise on both sides of the bread.

Place the cooked and sliced protein on the bottom half of the bread.

Top with pickled vegetables, fresh cilantro leaves, jalapeño slices, and sliced cucumber.

Drizzle with Maggi sauce or soy sauce for extra flavor.

Close the sandwich with the top half of the bread.

Serving:

Serve Banh Mi immediately and enjoy the delicious combination of flavors and textures!

Pair it with a refreshing Vietnamese iced coffee for an authentic experience.

Note: Banh Mi is versatile, so feel free to customize it with your favorite protein and additional toppings. Adjust the level of spice in the Sriracha mayonnaise to suit your taste. Maggi sauce adds a unique umami flavor, but you can substitute it with soy sauce if needed.

Satay Noodles

Ingredients:

For the Satay Sauce:

- 1/2 cup creamy peanut butter
- 3 tablespoons soy sauce
- 2 tablespoons hoisin sauce
- 2 tablespoons lime juice
- 2 tablespoons brown sugar
- 2 cloves garlic, minced
- 1 teaspoon grated ginger
- 1 teaspoon chili paste or Sriracha (adjust to taste)
- 1/2 cup coconut milk
- Water (as needed to adjust consistency)

For the Noodles:

- 8 oz (about 225g) rice noodles or egg noodles
- 2 tablespoons vegetable oil
- 1 cup broccoli florets
- 1 red bell pepper, thinly sliced
- 1 carrot, julienned
- 1 cup tofu, diced or protein of choice (chicken, shrimp, or beef)
- Chopped green onions and cilantro for garnish
- Crushed peanuts for topping

Instructions:

Making the Satay Sauce:

> In a bowl, whisk together peanut butter, soy sauce, hoisin sauce, lime juice, brown sugar, minced garlic, grated ginger, chili paste or Sriracha, and coconut milk. Adjust the consistency by adding water as needed. The sauce should be smooth and pourable.

Preparing the Noodles:

Cook the rice noodles or egg noodles according to the package instructions. Drain and set aside.

Stir-Frying the Ingredients:

Heat vegetable oil in a large pan or wok over medium-high heat.
Add diced tofu or protein of choice and cook until browned and cooked through.
Add broccoli florets, sliced red bell pepper, and julienned carrot to the pan. Stir-fry for 3-5 minutes until the vegetables are crisp-tender.
Add the cooked noodles to the pan and pour the satay sauce over the ingredients.
Toss everything together until well coated in the satay sauce and heated through.

Serving:

Transfer the satay noodles to serving plates.
Garnish with chopped green onions, cilantro, and crushed peanuts.
Serve immediately and enjoy the delicious and flavorful satay noodles!

Note: Feel free to customize the vegetables and protein based on your preferences.

Adjust the level of spiciness in the satay sauce to suit your taste. This dish can be made vegetarian by omitting the meat and using tofu or additional vegetables.

Japanese Takoyaki (Octopus Balls)

Ingredients:

For the Takoyaki Batter:

- 2 cups all-purpose flour
- 4 cups dashi stock (Japanese fish and seaweed stock)
- 4 large eggs
- 1/2 teaspoon salt
- 1/2 teaspoon soy sauce
- 1/2 teaspoon mirin (Japanese sweet rice wine)

For Filling:

- Cooked octopus, cut into small pieces
- Tenkasu (tempura scraps)
- Green onions, finely chopped
- Pickled red ginger (beni shoga)

For Toppings:

- Takoyaki sauce (store-bought or homemade)
- Japanese mayonnaise
- Aonori (dried green seaweed flakes)
- Katsuobushi (bonito flakes)

Instructions:

Making the Takoyaki Batter:

In a large bowl, whisk together all-purpose flour, dashi stock, eggs, salt, soy sauce, and mirin until the batter is smooth.
Let the batter rest for at least 30 minutes to allow any air bubbles to escape.

Cooking Takoyaki:

Preheat the takoyaki pan over medium-high heat. Brush each mold with vegetable oil.

Pour the takoyaki batter into each mold until it's almost full.

Place a piece of cooked octopus, some tenkasu, chopped green onions, and a bit of pickled red ginger into each mold.

Using takoyaki picks or skewers, start flipping the ingredients around to form a ball shape.

Continue turning the takoyaki balls until they are evenly cooked and golden brown on all sides.

Serving:

Transfer the takoyaki to a plate.

Drizzle with takoyaki sauce and Japanese mayonnaise.

Sprinkle aonori and katsuobushi on top.

Serve immediately while hot.

Note: Takoyaki pans with multiple molds are specifically designed for making this dish, but you can improvise with a cake pop maker if you don't have a takoyaki pan. Adjust the filling ingredients based on your preferences. Takoyaki is best enjoyed fresh and hot. Be cautious when flipping the takoyaki to avoid any burns.

Korean Street Toast

Ingredients:

For the Omelette:

- 2 large eggs
- Salt, to taste
- Black pepper, to taste
- 1 tablespoon butter

For the Toast:

- 4 slices of white bread
- Mayonnaise, to taste
- Ketchup, to taste
- Sugar, to taste
- American cheese slices
- Ham slices
- Fresh cabbage, thinly shredded
- Vegetable oil or butter for toasting

Optional Additions:

- Sausages
- Bacon
- Pickles

Instructions:

Preparing the Omelette:

Crack the eggs into a bowl, season with salt and black pepper, and whisk until well beaten.
Heat a non-stick pan over medium heat. Add butter to the pan and let it melt.
Pour the beaten eggs into the pan, swirling to create an even layer. Cook until the edges set and the bottom is cooked but still slightly runny.
Fold the omelette in half and continue cooking until it's fully cooked through. Set aside.

Assembling the Korean Street Toast:

- Spread mayonnaise on one side of each bread slice.
- Place a slice of American cheese on two slices of bread.
- Add a folded omelette on top of the cheese.
- Place ham slices on the omelette.
- Sprinkle a small amount of sugar over the ham.
- Add a layer of shredded cabbage on top.
- Drizzle ketchup over the cabbage.
- Close the sandwiches with the remaining slices of bread, mayonnaise side down.

Toasting the Sandwiches:

- Heat a pan or griddle over medium heat. Add a bit of vegetable oil or butter.
- Toast the sandwiches on both sides until the bread is golden brown and the cheese is melted.
- Press down on the sandwiches gently while toasting to help everything stick together.
- Remove from the pan and let them cool slightly before slicing.

Serving:

- Slice the Korean Street Toast diagonally into halves.
- Serve hot and enjoy the delicious and satisfying street toast!

Note: Feel free to customize the ingredients based on your preferences. You can add or omit elements to suit your taste. The combination of sweet and savory flavors makes this Korean street food classic a delightful treat.

www.ingramcontent.com/pod-product-compliance
Lightning Source LLC
LaVergne TN
LVHW081555060526
838201LV00054B/1892